Margaret Picton

Understanding Dress

Illustrated by Doreen Lang

BLACKIE

BLACKIE & SON LTD
Bishopbriggs . Glasgow G64 2NZ
•
Furnival House . 14–18 High Holborn . London WC1V 6BX

Printed in Great Britain by
Thomson Litho Ltd, East Kilbride, Scotland

Contents

Part One

About Fashion

CHAPTER 1

Why do we wear clothes?

Have you ever stopped to wonder why we wear clothes?
There are many reasons.

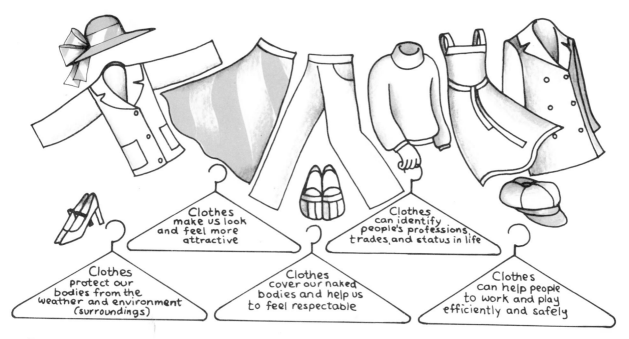

Clothes
make us look
and feel more
attractive

Clothes
can identify
people's professions,
trades, and status in life

Clothes
protect our
bodies from the
weather and environment
(surroundings)

Clothes
cover our naked
bodies and help us
to feel respectable

Clothes
can help people
to work and play
efficiently and safely

Let us consider each of these points. Clothes are
necessary to protect our bodies from the weather. In
winter we would soon feel cold, wet, and chapped without
the protection and comfort of waterproofed and warm
clothing. In a similar way the summer sun would dry,
crack, and blister our skin if we did not cover our bodies
with lightweight clothes. Shoes are needed to protect feet
from the hard ground. Headwear and gloves are sometimes
needed to shield the head and hands from extremes of
temperature.

The type of clothing we wear depends upon the climate
of the country in which we live. In very hot countries
people wear lightweight clothing that is loose and flowing.

This helps to keep their bodies cool. Examples can be found in the long, flowing saris worn by women in India, and the loose, voluminous robes of the bedouins in the hot deserts of Asia and Africa. Cotton, linen, silk, and some lightweight man-made materials (*not* nylon) are suitable for hot countries. They are cool to wear, they drape loosely, and they are easy to wash. White clothing is often worn in tropical climates because it cannot be bleached by the hot sun, nor does it absorb heat as quickly as coloured clothing. In very cold countries people wear thicker, warmer clothes. Wool, animal skins such as fur and leather, and heavy man-made materials are used. One example is the "parka" or long, hooded jacket worn by the Eskimos. This is made from animal skins. It is warm to wear and gives protection from wind, ice, and snow.

Clothes can make us look and feel attractive. It is always pleasant to be complimented on our appearance and to be well dressed gives us a feeling of self-confidence. A sensible person will choose styles and colours carefully to enhance good physical features and disguise bad ones. In Chapter 3 we will learn about good taste in clothes, and how to dress to suit one's own figure and colouring.

Our society considers it improper to be seen naked and so clothes are worn to cover the body. Apart from this practical usage, some clothes can have special significance. It is essential that people such as policemen and firemen are clearly recognizable and so a uniform is worn which makes them easy to identify. This is helpful to everybody.

Colour of clothing can be an identifying feature. The colour and style of a nurse's uniform clearly show the grade of nursing she has reached. Similarly, the colour, style of uniform, and type of decoration worn by members of the armed forces distinguish one rank from another. The colour of clothing used to have far more significance than it has today. In the seventeenth and eighteenth centuries, purple represented royalty and a scarlet robe denoted a judge. Serving men were dressed in blue and people in mourning wore only black. Today it is still conventional for a bride to wear white at her wedding. A baby girl is often dressed in pink, while a baby boy is dressed in blue, although these customs are slowly dying. Ermine, the white winter fur of the stoat, has long been a symbol of royalty and power. It is still used today in the coronation robes of kings and queens.

Some clothes give very special protection and ensure that people can work efficiently and safely. For example, labourers on building sites wear helmets to protect their heads from falling objects; astronauts wear spacesuits to protect them from the hazards of radiation; scientists wear overalls to protect their clothes from chemicals; deep-sea

divers wear special suits and breathing apparatus to help them to survive under the sea; steelworkers wear goggles to protect their eyes; surgeons wear sterile clothing when operating. Can you think of other examples of clothing that give a special type of protection?

Think and Do

1. Make a list of different types of protective clothing used for work and play.

2. Holidays are a comparatively recent custom.

a. Try to find out what clothing was worn on the beach at the beginning of this century.

b. Find out all you can on the origins of the bikini.

3. Why do you think chefs wear white aprons and hats when working in their kitchens?

4. Find out the current prices of:

a. a pair of wellington boots (your size);

b. a pair of polaroid sunglasses;

c. a nylon smock;

d. a good quality anorak or parka (your size);

e. a pair of household rubber gloves.

5. Imagine that you have been asked to design a new school uniform. What points would you consider to be important? Illustrate your answer, showing colours, styles, and types of fabric you would use.

6. Visit your school library and local public library and find out all you can about:

a. how the Eskimos dress;

b. spacesuits;

c. clothes worn at funerals in the nineteenth and twentieth centuries.

7. During Easter weekend you are planning to go on a ramble, staying overnight in youth hostels. What clothing and footwear would you take?

8. Why do we wear clothes? Illustrate your answer with drawings, magazine pictures, photographs, etc.

9. Choose a word from Column B to complete each sentence in Column A. Write out the completed sentences.

Column A   *Column B*

a. A . . . . . . is a long, flowing robe   *cotton*
   worn by Indian women.
b. . . . . . . is a cool fabric to wear.   *parka*
c. . . . . . . clothing does not absorb
   heat as quickly as coloured clothing.   *chemicals*
d. A . . . . . . is a long, hooded jacket
   made from fur and animal skins.   *black*
e. An astronaut's suit protects him
   from . . . . . .   *wool*
f. . . . . . . is the colour associated with
   mourning.   *sari*
g. . . . . . . is a fabric often used for
   winter clothing.   *radiation*
h. A scientist wears an overall to pro-
   tect his clothes and skin from   *white*
   . . . . . .

10. Make a list of all the people you can think of with occupations or professions that are denoted by the colour and style of their clothing.

Clothes through the ages

The first body coverings consisted of fur and animal skins, which were simply draped around the body. Early men then discovered that sharp bones could be used as needles, and animal sinews or strips of leather as thread, and so the first clothes were fashioned.

In the Bronze Age, men learned how to make cloth by spinning thread from the wool of sheep and goats and weaving it on a loom. Linen was also made, from the flax plant. The first clothes were very simple in design and usually consisted of a loose tunic, belted around the waist. Bronze Age men wore leather breeches, tied in a criss-cross pattern, with simple cloaks of coarse wool across their shoulders. Bronze Age women wore belted woollen tunics over *kirtles* or underdresses. Blankets were used as simple cloaks.

Men then learned how to colour cloth by using natural dyes taken from fruits, plants, and animals. Stripes and checks became popular and clothes brighter. Simple buttons were carved from jet, and sometimes ornamental pins were used to fasten garments together. The Ancient Britons became more skilled at spinning, weaving, and dyeing, and by the time of the Roman conquest of Britain fine cloth was being made. British chiefs wore bright clothes to make them look important, and class distinction in style of dress was already apparent. Tunic-like costumes were still worn but men covered their tunics and breeches with hooded cloaks, while women used to drape blankets over their shoulders. Shoes were worn by this time, either moccasins or sandals.

Rough woollens and linens continued to be used for clothes during the age of the Saxons, but rich people wore cloaks and tunics embroidered in gold thread and trimmed with ermine and squirrel fur. Saxon tunics had long, tight, wrinkled sleeves. These could be pulled down to keep the hands warm if necessary.

After the Norman Conquest, the differences between the dress of the wealthy and the poor became more apparent. The rich wore well-fitting, brightly coloured garments made from fine wool, linen, and silk, but the peasants still wore loose clothes which were dull in colour and made from heavy wool or canvas.

In the twelfth and thirteenth centuries men's clothes became shorter and the tunic and outer coat (*surcote*) were slit up the front to make walking and riding easier. Cloaks with small, closely fitting caps or hoods were popular. Loose-fitting underpants called *braies* were worn either with or without stockings. Gloves were introduced during this period. Women wore long kirtles with trains that would sweep the floor. Their heads were covered with veils, and *wimples* were draped under their chins and fastened above the ears. This style of head-dress was very popular. Rich ladies might choose to wear their hair in two long plaits, braided with ribbon, and use make-up to enhance their looks. Clothes during this period were simple, functional, and often quite severe in line.

During the fourteenth and fifteenth centuries dress became more colourful and extravagant. Rich men wore long gowns with wide sleeves, or short, pleated top-coats edged with fur. It became fashionable to pad out the chest and pull the waist in tightly with a belt. Coloured stockings were worn, and long pointed shoes. Poor people still dressed in rough, belted tunics and wore clogs or thick shoes. The *capuchon* was a head-dress worn by both rich and poor. It consisted of a short cape and hood, and could be worn with a tunic or cloak. Ladies of this period wore long, full dresses and underdresses. Their head-dresses were tall and very elaborate. Pointed hats, with a fur roll around the crown or a long veil, were popular. Peasant women wore long, simple dresses with either a hood or a wimple and veil. During this period laws were passed to forbid poor people to wear bright colours, fur, jewels and fine cloth, and so the difference in dress between rich and poor became more pronounced.

In Tudor England, men's dress became broader and more manly. Rich men wore suits of silk, velvet, or brocade, decorated with jewels. Sleeves were padded and often slashed to show a silken shirt. Short, padded breeches were fashionable, worn with velvet stockings and wide, open shoes. Bright colours were preferred, scarlet and green being very popular. Poor men still dressed in plain clothes of coarse wool or unbleached linen, and slashing was forbidden to them by law. Tudor ladies wore heavy dresses of velvet or brocade, with loosely draped or winged sleeves. Bodices were tight and the overdress was usually slit in front to show a richly embroidered underdress. Stiff, arch-shaped head-dresses were fashionable. Poor women wore aprons over short-skirted dresses. White caps or thin strips of material would cover their hair.

In Elizabeth's reign costume became stiffer, more awkward to wear, and very heavily decorated. Elizabethan men and women wore *ruffs* or starched collars. These were usually made of white cambric, and were heavily pleated, starched, and held in place by wires. They must have been very uncomfortable to wear. Rich men wore padded breeches, tightly fitting tunics or **doublets** and velvet cloaks. Slashing was still used as a means of decoration and the silk, velvet, or brocade clothes could have jewels sewn on them. Knitted stockings were now fashionable. Poor men wore loose, belted doublets over plain shirts. Tight bodices and very full skirts were worn by ladies of this period. A wired underskirt called a *farthingale* was used to hold out the overdresses. Padded sleeves and rich embroidery were popular. Ordinary women wore woollen dresses and kirtles in dull colours.

Cotton was not used for weaving into cloth until after 1600, when the manufacture of cotton goods became an important industry centred around Lancashire. In the seventeenth century clothes became less bulky. The Elizabethan ruff disappeared and was replaced by the lace collar. During this period men wore loose trousers which fastened at the knee, doublets, and cloaks. Wide-brimmed hats trimmed with feathers were popular. Later in this era men's costume changed, and long coats with waistcoats and breeches became fashionable. This was the beginning of modern dress. Wigs were worn and gentlemen of fashion would carry a sword. Ladies of this period wore high-waisted, low-necked gowns of stiff silk or satin, trimmed with lace. Farthingales were no longer worn and the *fontange* style of head-dress—a towering, wired, lace cap—was popular.

During the eighteenth century costume became more sober. This century marked the return towards "classical" lines in clothing, the aim being refinement and daintiness in everything. Knee-breeches gave way to trousers, tightly fitting coats were replaced by loose frock-coats, and the sleeved waistcoat became the shorter, sleeveless version that is known today. Wigs were worn by most men, and starched neckcloths or *cravats* became popular. A great change also took place in women's fashion. At first dresses were made of heavy, rich materials and their full skirts were stretched over hooped petticoats. Low necks were fashionable and ornamental panels called *stomachers* were often inserted in the front bodice. At the turn of the century more flimsy materials were used and styles became simpler. High-waisted dresses with narrow skirts were worn, and the tall, elaborate hairstyles that had been popular were replaced by shorter, curlier styles. Tall ostrich-feathers were worn as hair decorations. In this era poor men wore knee-breeches, shirts, and stout woollen stockings. Short, sleeveless waistcoats worn with spotted neckerchiefs became popular. Simple serviceable garments such as linen smocks were worn by farm workers. Plain gowns, aprons, and mob caps continued to be the garb of working women.

In Victorian England, men's clothes became quieter in colour. It was felt that dark, sober colours were more fitting for a practical age; "the reign of drabness" in men's clothing had begun. Tight trousers strapped under the foot became the fashion. Coats varied in length and style from the tail-coat and frock-coat to the morning-coat, which was only worn on very formal occasions. Overcoats were either short and loose or long and fitted. Some over-

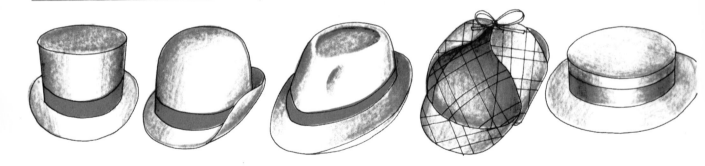

coats had an attached cape. The *macintosh* appeared during this period and so did the *norfolk jacket* with *knickerbockers*. Top hats and tall felt bowlers were popular, but the deerstalker and Homburg became fashionable towards the end of the nineteenth century. By the end of the Victorian era men's clothes had become very much like our present-day styles.

In 1851 the first sewing machine was made and this heralded a great change in the clothing industry. Housewives could now make clothes for their families, and factories specializing in mass-produced garments became widespread. This led to more reasonably priced clothes.

For women the age of the wide skirt and *crinoline* had arrived. Victorian ladies had "hour-glass" figures, their dresses being wide at the shoulders, tiny at the well-corseted waists, and very wide in the skirts. Several layers of petticoats were worn at first to achieve this effect, but later the hooped petticoat or caged crinoline was invented. Evening dresses were low cut and worn off the shoulders. Shawls, bonnets, muffs, and caps were fashionable and Victorian ladies wore gloves to keep their hands soft, even at night. The *bustle* followed the crinoline. It consisted of a pad and cushion worn at the back to hold out the skirt. *Leg-of-mutton* sleeves were popular and the *dolman* cloak or shawl was a favourite outdoor garment. By the end of the nineteenth century the bustle had disappeared and plain, flared, long skirts, worn with blouses, became the fashion. By 1900, suits consisting of a long skirt and jacket were the vogue. These were usually worn with straw *boater* hats.

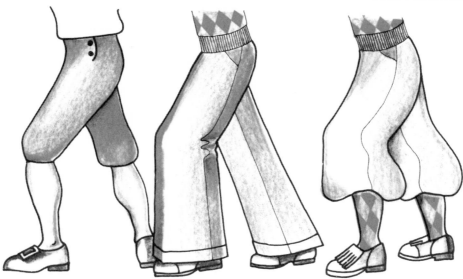

In the twentieth century men's trouser bottoms developed turn-ups. Then very wide trousers called *Oxford bags* became the rage. *Plus-fours,* a type of knicker-bocker pouched below the knee, were worn on sporting occasions. Gradually the frock-coat was discarded, and men's dress became much more informal. Lounge suits, tweed jackets with sports trousers, and soft felt hats became popular. Men's fashion returned briefly to the Edwardian era with the "Teddy boy" look, but this and other dramatic changes have been only temporary. At the beginning of the twentieth century women wore skirts with trains that swept the floor. Walking became even more difficult with the *hobble* skirt, a long, very tight skirt that severely restricted movement. Then fashions became gradually shorter. Women seemed to rebel against uncomfortable clothing, and loose, short dresses with low waists became the fashion.

This change came about when women started to lead a more active outdoor life. The First World War found many women working in munitions factories, offices, and on the land; their need was for simple, sensible styles of clothing that were practical to wear. The *cloche* hat was the vogue, and hair was worn very short. Slacks and shorts were first worn in the 1930s. The Second World

War marked a return to austerity in women's fashion, but after the war the "New Look" was born, and dresses and coats became longer, flared, and more feminine. This century has also seen the "Mini", the "Maxi", and the "Midi" when hem lines rose and dropped dramatically. The first seventy years of this century have witnessed many changes in fashion, but today's clothes seem to have assumed a casual, easy-to-wear character.

Think and Do

1. Select any period in British history and write an illustrated account of the dress worn at that time.

2. Copy the following sentences into your notebook. Say whether each one is *true* or *false*.

a. A kirtle was an underdress.

b. Saxon tunics had short, loose sleeves.

c. The dolman was a type of cloak.

d. Hooped petticoats were used to widen the skirts of dresses in the nineteenth century.

e. A farthingale was a head-dress popular in the seventeenth century.

f. The first buttons were carved from jet.

g. With the "New Look", women started to wear longer and more feminine styles in clothing.

h. The term "leg-of-mutton" was used to describe a type of trouser in Victorian England.

3. On which parts of the body were the following worn?

a. Surcote
b. Moccasins
c. Braies
d. Breeches
e. Ruff
f. Doublet
g. Farthingale
h. Fontange
i. Stomacher
j. Knickerbockers
k. Boater
l. Deerstalker

4. The illustration shows examples of the "Mini", "Maxi", and "Midi" styles in women's fashion. In your notebook, say which you like best and give reasons for your choice.

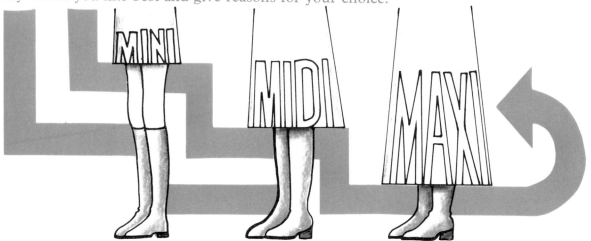

5. Prepare a classroom frieze on "Clothes through the ages".

6. Rearrange the following letters. They are all items of men's clothing.

a. EUTDOBL
b. CATRAV
c. OFDRXO BGAS
d. RIBSAE
e. UNCHAPOC
f. ULPS ORUSF

7. Copy out this crossword and complete it.

Clues across

1. This was worn around the neck in Elizabethan England.
2. A lady's head-covering popular in the twelfth and thirteenth centuries.
3. The first clothes were shaped like this.
4. Early man used these to make needles.

Clues down

5. This consists of a pad and cushion.
6. . . . . . . is made from the flax plant.
7. Poor people were forbidden to wear this.
8. A lady's hat of the twentieth century.

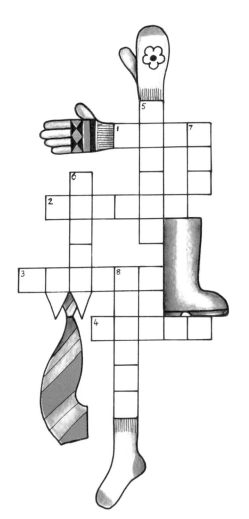

8. Describe in your own words the main fashion trends for the current year.

9. Try to find out when:

a. knitting was introduced and first used for stockings;
b. starch was first used to stiffen clothes.

10. Ask your parents and grandparents to describe the type of clothing they used to wear: *a.* for school; *b.* on a Sunday. How have styles and fabrics changed since their childhood?

What shall we wear?

Most people would like to look and feel attractive. That is one of the reasons we wear clothes. Unfortunately not all clothes help us in this aim. Some clothes make us look fat, and some clothes have the opposite effect. Most styles in clothing are more suited to one type of figure than to another. It is important therefore that we take a good look in the mirror and decide upon the good and bad points about our own figure. We can then use this knowledge to choose the styles and colours that will suit us best. If we dress sensibly we can enhance our good features and help to disguise our bad ones.

Here are some fashion tips to help tall people look their best.

Always walk tall, with your back straight and your head held high. If you stoop or slouch in an effort to look shorter you will only make yourself look awkward and ungainly.

Do not wear vertically striped or patterned materials. Horizontal or diagonal stripes are more becoming, but do remember that horizontal stripes add width, so these are only for the very slim.

Try to create the illusion of width by using chunky fabrics or big, bold patterns. A hairstyle should give width to the face and not be too severe or closely cropped.

Do not wear tight, clinging clothes. These will make you look even taller. The layered look and soft, full overdresses are definitely for you.

Try to ''break up'' your height. A belted dress, a skirt and top, trousers with a sweater, will all help to do this.

Short people can also use clothes to their advantage if the following golden rules are observed.

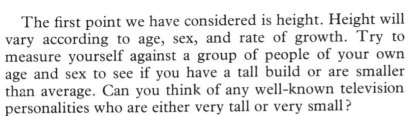

Vertically striped or patterned materials will add height. V-necks and vertical seaming can help with this illusion.

A hat should give you height, not width, so avoid wide-brimmed creations. Keep hair-styles short and neat.

Try not to "break up" your height with wide belts or low waistlines. These all send the eye outwards instead of upwards. Do not wear three-quarter length coats, jackets, or jerkins.

Styles should be simple. A neat, trim appearance is most becoming for you. Avoid big collars, bold patterns, and styles which have layers. Do not wear fussy frills.

Outfits in one colour, or toning separates, are right for you.

Fabrics should be smooth to emphasise your slimness. Thick, chunky materials that give the impression of width should be avoided.

The first point we have considered is height. Height will vary according to age, sex, and rate of growth. Try to measure yourself against a group of people of your own age and sex to see if you have a tall build or are smaller than average. Can you think of any well-known television personalities who are either very tall or very small?

The next point we will consider is width. Some people are fat, but many people who think of themselves as fat are just badly proportioned. They may have a normal bust measurement for their height but have heavy hips and thighs, or they may be bigger than average around the bust but have normal waist and hip measurements. Average body widths will vary with age and sex. The measurement standard committee of the pattern industry has produced the following table as a guide to pre-teen and teen figures.

Size code	9/10	11/12	13/14	15/16	
Bust (cm)	78	81	85	89	
Waist (cm)	61	64	66	69	
Hip (cm)	85	89	93	97	

This table gives measurements for the average, well-proportioned Misses' figure.

Size code	10	12	14	16	18
Bust (cm)	83	87	92	97	102
Waist (cm)	64	67	71	76	81
Hip (cm)	88	92	97	102	107

Ask a friend to help you check your bust, waist, and hip measurements against those given in the relevant chart. When taking body measurements, draw the tape measure close but not tight, and measure on top of your normal underclothes.

If you are heavily out of proportion in any measurement then help to disguise this by wearing good, well-fitting foundation garments. You should start to wear a bra as soon as your bust begins to develop. Bras are bought by the normal bust measurement in inches, e.g. 32, 34, 36, or the under-bust measurement in 5 cm intervals, e.g. 70, 75, 80. When choosing a bra you will also need to know what size of cup suits you best. If you have a small bust, choose an AA or A cup. An average-sized bust will need a B cup. A large bust will need a C cup, and larger, fuller busts are catered for with D and DD cup sizes. The label on the bra will show a series of numbers and letters,

A bust measurement should be taken around the fullest part of the bust going high under the arm but straight across the back

A waist measurement should follow the natural waistline

A hip measurement is taken around the fullest part of the hip, usually 18cm below the waistline for young junior/teenagers and 23cm below the waistline for misses e.g.

A well-fitting bra should:
  a give support and keep the bust firm;
  b fit comfortably and not leave red weals on the
     shoulders or under the bust.

To be well dressed and look smart you should always
have a flat stomach. Cultivate the habit of pulling your
tummy in flat, and try to develop a good posture. If you
feel that you need extra support, especially when wearing
figure-hugging clothes, try buying stretch pantees or a
light, elastic panti-girdle. Elastic girdles are bought by the
normal waist measurement in inches, e.g. 25–26, 27–28,
and in 5 cm intervals, e.g. 65, 70. The label will look like
this:

It is also possible to disguise out-of-proportion measurements by wearing the right clothes. Here is a chart to help
you.

Fault	How to help
1. Large bust	Choose a bra that gives plenty of support. You will probably need a C cup. Avoid wearing clothes that are tight across the bust. This will emphasize your problem. A loose blouse or draped dress-top is more becoming. Do not wear "fussy" necklines. Remember that vertical stripes are slimming, but do not wear big, bold patterns. Dark colours are slimming but do avoid shiny materials. If you are lucky and have small or average-sized hips, show them off by wearing neatly fitting skirts or trousers.
2. Large hips	Stretch pantees or a light elastic girdle will help. Do not wear dresses or skirts that are very full around the hips. Remember that if you wear tightly fitting trousers, this will only accentuate your problem. A simple, classic style in trousers will suit you best. Avoid horizontally striped fabrics, big or bold patterns, and shiny materials. If you have a small or average-sized bust, try to focus attention there by wearing pretty tops.
3. Small bust	A bra with an A cup will suit you best. Bodices that have gathering, pin-tucks, or draping across the bust are helpful.
4. Small hips	Trousers and fitted skirts and dresses suit you best. Do not hide your slimness in very full skirts.

If you can class yourself as an average-sized person then you are lucky. Most styles, fashions, and materials will suit you.

The next point we will consider is colouring. Fair-haired people with fair skins can wear most colours successfully. Rich shades of blue are particularly becoming. People with sallow (yellow-toned) skins look best in bright colours. Gay, clear shades of red, blue, and green are flattering. Muddy, indefinite colours should be avoided, and cold colours such as lemon and primrose are not suitable. A splash of white near the face will tend to lighten a sallow skin. High-coloured complexions can be softened by wearing neutral or cool colours such as grey, green, or blue. Bright, hot colours only emphasize a florid complexion and should be avoided. Auburn-haired people can wear greens and blues successfully, and red-heads look best in soft, muted colours such as moss green. Do remember that:

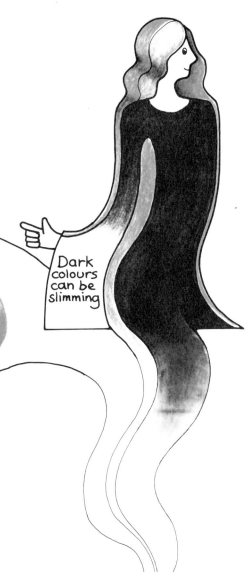

Each year different colours seem to be fashionable, and it is fun to try out new and unusual shades. Do be sensible, though, and if the latest fashion colour definitely does not suit your colouring then limit yourself to small splashes of the colour, worn well away from the face. This can be done by using the colour for accessories such as handbags and shoes, or for decorative features such as braiding, embroidery, belts, and pockets.

When choosing a garment, try to visualize it as part of an outfit. Accessories can make or mar the picture and should always be chosen with care. Scarves, handbags, gloves, and shoes can blend or tone with the garments worn, or they can form a contrast in colour and texture. Bold primary colours are suitable for accessories. They are often safer and more becoming when worn in small amounts in this way. Do not make the mistake of choosing accessories in different tones of the same colour. This can be disastrous. Always take a colour sample with you when buying matching accessories. Check that accessories such as handbags balance with the line of the other garments. For example, a tiny, smart-looking handbag does not look right when worn with jeans and a chunky sweater. A casual shoulder bag will look more appropriate.

Footwear is an expensive but necessary item of clothing, and should be chosen with care. Here are some general points to help you when buying shoes/boots/sandals, etc.
1 Footwear should be suitable for the occasion. A sensible person would not choose flimsy sandals for a country ramble, nor choose strong walking shoes for a fashionable party.

2 Winter footwear should give protection from the weather. Be wary of fashionable boots which are often delightful to look at but not waterproof.

3 Everyday shoes should be comfortable to wear and give support to the feet.

4 "Dressy" shoes should not be too high. Thick platform soles and very high heels are bad for the posture. The body is tilted forward unnaturally, and permanent damage can be caused to the spine if these kinds of shoes are worn continually. *Be warned!*

5 Choose low- or medium-heeled sandals/shoes when wearing trousers. Very high-heeled shoes can be dangerous if the heel accidentally gets caught in the hem.

6 Always buy the best that you can afford, when choosing footwear. If you are not satisfied with the wear you have received from a recent purchase, do return them to the shop and make a complaint.

7 Do not rush to buy the latest style. Stop first, and ask yourself:

    a   do I really need them?
    b   are they suitable for my needs?
    c   do they seem comfortable to wear?
    d   do they seem to be well made?
    e   do I really like them?
    f   can I afford them?

If all the answers are "yes", then you will be making a sensible purchase.

8 Footwear should fit neatly around the heel. Toes should not feel tight or pinched, and there should be no ridges anywhere to cause blisters, corns, or bunions.

9 Always try on items of footwear. Never buy by size alone. Sizes and widths vary with different makes, and it is important to check that shoes fit correctly before leaving the shop.

The sensible teenager who knows how to dress to suit her figure and colouring will have few problems in choosing a suitable outfit for each different occasion. Today's range of separates and mix-and-match fashion pieces makes planning a wardrobe exciting. There are fewer restrictions and rules of etiquette concerning dress than was the case only a generation ago, and the modern girl has a freedom of choice that her Edwardian counterpart would have envied. Even so, it is best to bear in mind a few simple rules when dressing to suit an occasion, and here are some general points to help you.

NOTICE

If overalls are worn, choose ones that are simple in style and easy to wash. They should be fairly loose, giving ease of movement around the neck and under the arms. Remember that high-necked styles with long sleeves may be warm in winter but hot and uncomfortable in summer.

CHOOSING CLOTHES FOR WORK

A neat, workmanlike appearance should be your aim. Styles should be simple. Do not wear extremes of fashion—save these for your leisure activities.

Pockets, belts, and cuffs should be small, so that there is no danger of clothing catching on doors, cupboards, or parts of machinery.

If there is no standard uniform which you must wear, choose something comfortable, hard-wearing, and easy to wash.

Dark colours are more practical than light colours. They will not show the dirt so easily.

Avoid wearing expensive or "flashy" jewellery. This is not suitable for work.

CHOOSING CLOTHES FOR LEISURE

Wear suitable clothing for outdoor activities—"whites" for tennis, anoraks and stout shoes for rambling, jodhpurs for riding.

Choose clothes that will drip dry.

Leisure clothes should be comfortable to wear. They should help to give you a relaxed feeling.

Even old favourites should be kept in good condition; do not let clothes deteriorate.

Slacks, jeans, skirts, and tops are suitable.

Leisure clothes should be easy to wash, but should also be in a colour and fabric that will not show the dirt.

HOW TO DRESS FOR AN INTERVIEW

Do not wear anything which is too short or too long. Avoid tight clothing that makes you aware of your figure.

Tights or stockings must not be laddered. Check that they do not wrinkle round the ankles.

Wear suitable accessories —sensible but smart shoes, a neat handbag. A hat is not essential, but wear one if you feel comfortable in it.

Avoid unnecessary jewellery.

Choose a simple, neat hairstyle. Use make-up sparingly and look clean and immaculate.

Do not wear anything too fashionable. This may make you feel uncomfortable and self-conscious.

A smart suit or matching dress and jacket would be very suitable. A trouser suit or neat skirt with matching co-ordinates would be equally appropriate.

HOW TO DRESS FOR A FUNERAL

Choose a dark outfit of clothes. It is not necessary to wear black.

Wear neat, formal styles. Avoid fashionable clothes that might look flippant and frivolous.

A hat is no longer essential, but should be worn if you feel comfortable in one.

Avoid unnecessary jewellery.

HOW TO DRESS FOR A WEDDING

Choose smart, comfortable shoes. It may be a long day, so "pinching" shoes with too high a heel are definitely out!

Check that your ensemble is seasonable. It would not be very sensible to shiver your way through a winter wedding in a light-weight chiffon creation!

Choose a gay outfit in a bright colour. Weddings are usually happy occasions, and clothes should help to convey this feeling.

Gloves are not essential, but they can help to complete an outfit.

Wear a hat to complete your ensemble—something fancy, frivolous, and fashionable.

CHOOSING CLOTHES FOR A HOLIDAY

Plan your holiday wardrobe with the expected climate in mind. You will need different clothes for a skiing holiday from those you would need for a Mediterranean sun-spot.

Remember to pack some warm clothing, even for a summer holiday. Evenings can be very cool.

You will need some "dressy" outfits, so do not take only casual clothes.

Do not forget to pack sun glasses, sun hats, and a pretty head-scarf. You may also need a mackintosh, so be prepared!

If you are planning a beach holiday, take several bathing costumes. A range of T-shirts, shorts, and beach cover-up garments will also be useful.

Clothes that can be easily washed are necessary for a holiday wardrobe. Drip-dry outfits are a bonus.

Choose clothes that can be easily packed into a suitcase. Crease-resistant man-made fabrics are excellent for this purpose.

Being well dressed does not end with wearing the right clothes and accessories. A smart, attractive person gives much thought and care to the basic essentials of good grooming.

Make-up is used sparingly but cleverly. She has experimented to find the colour of foundation, blusher, and lipstick that suits her best. Eye shadow and mascara have been applied lightly, and lipstick blotted.

Her hair looks healthy and well-groomed, with no sign of dandruff.

Nails are manicured to give a clean, neat appearance.

She is particular about personal hygiene, washing hair, face, and body regularly. Deodorants and anti-perspirants are used as often as necessary.

She is wearing clean tights [or stockings or socks] without any holes or ladders, and clean, fresh underclothes.

She cleans and flosses her teeth regularly, and pays frequent visits to the dentist for check-ups. This helps guard against tooth and gum decay, and bad breath.

She uses a good cleansing cream to keep her skin fresh and free from spots.

Clothes look clean and well pressed. Buttons are firmly sewn on and hems are level.

She keeps her figure trim and in good shape, wearing foundation garments if necessary.

Shoes are clean and in good condition. Any necessary repairs have been dealt with straight away.

Think and Do

1. What advice would you give to a young teenager on buying footwear? Illustrate your answer with examples of shoes which are good and bad for the feet.

2. Have fun creating "Ascot" type hats from coloured paper, scraps of lace, net, foil, feathers, etc. Arrange a competition to find the best creations in the following groups:
a. the most unusual;
b. the most outrageous;
c. the most dignified.
3. How should a tall, slim, young girl dress? List six points that she should consider when choosing clothes.
4. Prepare a classroom display on make-up. Ask your teacher if she can arrange a talk and demonstration by a trained beautician on the correct use of cosmetics.
5. Decide on a colour for each of the following outfits and then describe and draw suitable accessories for each one.

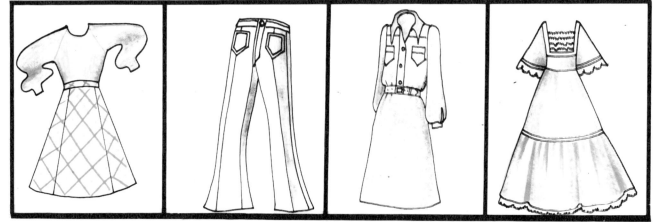

6. Find out the current price of:
a. a lightweight panti-girdle;
b. a bra slip;
c. a short wedding veil;
d. a pair of fashion boots;
e. a good-quality lipstick;
f. a denim or suede shoulder bag;
g. a pair of evening shoes;
h. a bottle of nail varnish.
7. Imagine that you have been invited to attend an interview for a secretarial post. Sketch and describe an outfit of clothes you think would be suitable to wear for the occasion. Give reasons for your choice.

8. Look through newspapers, magazines, and photograph albums and find pictures of weddings. Try to include some wedding groups from different eras. Choose your favourite wedding dress and give reasons for your choice.

9. Look through magazines and try to find pictures of outfits which you would recommend for each of the following:

a. a Christmas shopping expedition;

b. a day's hike;

c. the annual office dinner and dance;

d. a visit to the theatre;

e. a night at the local disco club;

f. a day on the beach in mid-summer;

g. a family wedding;

h. a local football match.

10. Copy out the following crossword and complete it.

Clues across

1. Vertical . . . . . . are slimming.

2. A cold colour.

3. A range of clothes which mix and match well.

Clues down

4. This gives support.

5. A measurement taken about 20 cm below the waist.

6. Items that complete an outfit.

Planning a wardrobe

It is only when you first start to buy your own clothes that you realize how expensive they are. Do budget your income to allow for clothing. It is not easy to say what proportion of an income should be spent on clothing, because this will vary from person to person, and family to family. For example, a teenager who has just started work and has a minimum of expenses will be able to spend more on clothing for herself than a housewife who has to spread her clothing allowance to cover other members of the family. When planning a clothing budget, put aside a certain sum of money in savings each week. A teenager can use a bank or building society for her regular savings. It is not a good idea to leave money around the house or in a handbag. A housewife may choose to use her weekly child benefit allowance for her children's clothes. This can be left to accumulate until there is sufficient to buy the clothing needed.

Some people order clothes from mail order catalogues. Mail order firms offer a wide range of clothes which can be bought with credit facilities, or returned if not suitable. Prices are often higher than in the shops because of the expenses involved in advertising, postage and packing, etc. This method of buying clothes is worth considering if you prefer to pay in instalments. If ordering clothes from a mail order catalogue, do:

> *a* remember to allocate money each week for the repayments;
> *b* guard against ordering too many items at once.

When choosing clothes it is a good idea to include several basic essentials, such as well-cut skirts and trousers. These can be worn with a range of accessories, which will help to add variety to your wardrobe. Separates, co-ordinates, and mix-and-match fashion pieces, are ideal for the teenager, who can interchange her outfits to suit the occasion, climate, and mood. For example, the range of accessories below illustrates the different combinations that can be worn with a good, basic skirt.

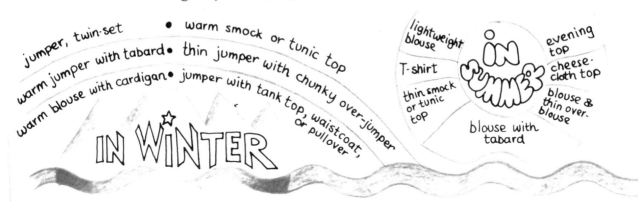

jumper, twin-set • warm smock or tunic top
warm jumper with tabard • thin jumper with chunky over-jumper
warm blouse with cardigan • jumper with tank top, waistcoat, or pullover

IN WINTER

lightweight blouse
T-shirt
thin smock or tunic top
blouse with tabard
evening top
cheese-cloth top
blouse & thin over-blouse

As fashion changes, other combinations or possibilities are revealed, and for the teenager who plans her wardrobe choosing clothes can be exciting.

Here are some general points to help you when planning a wardrobe and buying clothes.

1 It is a good idea to make a list of your needs. Put the main items at the top of the list.

Making a list will guard against rash & impulsive buying

CLOTHES NEEDED
WINTER COAT
JUMPER
~~~~~~~
~~~~~
~~~~ ~~~~
BRA SLIP
2 PRS. PANTIES
EVENING SHOES
~~~~~~

Try to estimate how much you will require for each item. If you have not allowed enough ask yourself if any of your needs can wait a little longer.

Do not forget to include underwear and footwear

Coats and suits are likely to be the most expensive items in your wardrobe, and should always be of good quality. It is false economy to try to save money by buying cheap versions which will quickly look worn and shabby.

2 It is not wise to buy a coat or suit in the very latest style. Fashion changes quickly and you might find that last year's brand-new ultra-fashionable coat is completely wrong for this season. Try to choose "safe" styles that do not date, and remember that plain, neutral colours can be teamed with a variety of different accessories, whereas gaudy, patterned clothes do not mix and match easily.

3 When buying new clothes, try to pick items that will combine with existing clothes. This will help to create a more varied wardrobe.

4 Try to plan your wardrobe so that several expensive items are not needed in the same year. For example, if you require a new winter coat, then postpone buying a new suit until the following year. Try instead to rejuvenate your old suit by buying new accessories.

5 Do not buy rashly or impulsively. This type of purchase is often regretted at leisure.

6 Always try on ready-made clothes before buying. If this is not possible, make sure that the garment can be exchanged if not suitable, or your money refunded. Many large department stores allow customers to exchange items at any of their branches, or they give a money-back guarantee. This is a valuable service for the shopper and is worth considering when deciding where to buy clothes.

7 Do "window shop" before you buy. Compare prices at several shops before you finally make a decision. Feel the quality of the fabric and inspect the finish of the garment. A well-made garment will have:

    a plaids, checks, or patterns matched at the seams;
    b generous seam and hem allowances;
    c well-finished seams;
    d facings and openings that lie flat;
    e smooth, even stitching that does not pull or pucker at the seams.

The garment should hang and fit correctly. There should be room for movement under the arms, and the neckline should lie flat.

A word about sales

When buying sales goods, always look for a good trade

name. If you are buying a reduced own-brand product from a reputable store, then it is likely to be an end-of-season reduction or a discontinued line. These are usually genuine bargains, and the discerning shopper will not hesitate to buy them. Be wary of cheap-quality goods that do not have a trade or brand name. Many items of clothing are sold as "sale bargains" when they are really cheaply produced goods which have been made especially for the sales. They are often of a cheap-quality fabric, and are skimpy in width and seam allowance. These should be avoided.

Home dressmaking

Some people like to economize by making clothes at home. Home dressmaking is fun and if you have the time available, it is worth considering making at least a few of the items needed in your wardrobe. An inexperienced dressmaker should start with the specially easy-to-make patterns produced by the well-known pattern firms. As skill and proficiency improve, the home dressmaker will want to attempt more complicated patterns.

Always look for a good-quality fabric, if you are making clothes yourself. It can be heartbreaking to spend time and money on a garment only to find that it does not wash or wear well. (On page 102, Chapter 11, you will find some helpful hints for choosing fabrics.)

Sometimes cut-out and ready-to-sew garments can be purchased from fashion magazines. The garments come in a kit complete with sewing instructions and the necessary trimmings. Dressmaking processes such as bound button-holes and stiffened belts may already have been done, to help give that professional look to your finished garment. These kits are worth considering, if you happen to like the particular style and fabric being offered. The finished garment may be more expensive than a similar garment made from your own choice of fabric, but it must be remembered that there is no wastage of material and that the ready-to-sew pattern pieces do save on time and labour. Can you think of any more advantages and disadvantages of ready-to-sew clothes?

Clothing a family

Many home dressmakers like to make clothes for babies and young children. The size of the garments makes them easy to handle, and they are often simple and quick to make. When clothing a baby or young child there are several points to consider.

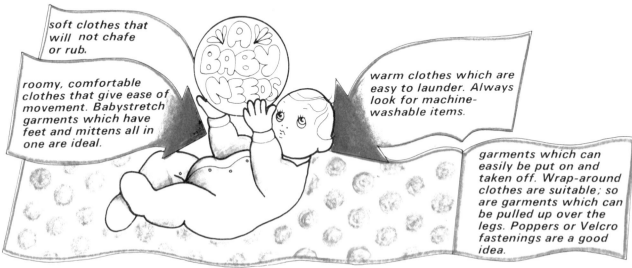

A BABY NEEDS

soft clothes that will not chafe or rub.

roomy, comfortable clothes that give ease of movement. Babystretch garments which have feet and mittens all in one are ideal.

warm clothes which are easy to launder. Always look for machine-washable items.

garments which can easily be put on and taken off. Wrap-around clothes are suitable; so are garments which can be pulled up over the legs. Poppers or Velcro fastenings are a good idea.

A TODDLER OR VERY YOUNG CHILD NEEDS

clothes that will wash easily and require little or no ironing. Always look for machine-washable items.

lightweight clothing that will not weigh him or her down.

sleep-suits or pyjamas whose top and bottom button together.

drip-dry, crease-resistant garments which are colour-fast and pre-shrunk.

comfortable clothes that give ease of movement. Tight, restricting belts are not necessary at this age.

attractive, sturdy garments that wear well.

shoes which fit in length, width, and girth. Toes should lie flat, but there should be room for growth. Check that shoes fit comfortably round the heel.

warm, one-piece garments that will not come apart at the waist.

non-inflammable garments.

As a child grows older, fashion becomes more important. He/she will want to have a say when choosing clothes, and the sensible parent will appreciate this. Advice and guidance can be given to help the child to develop good taste in clothing.

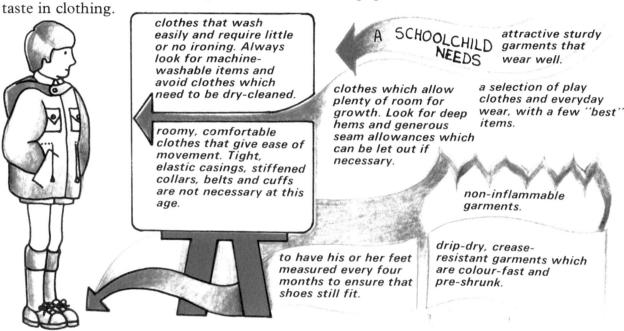

A SCHOOLCHILD NEEDS

clothes that wash easily and require little or no ironing. Always look for machine-washable items and avoid clothes which need to be dry-cleaned.

roomy, comfortable clothes that give ease of movement. Tight, elastic casings, stiffened collars, belts and cuffs are not necessary at this age.

clothes which allow plenty of room for growth. Look for deep hems and generous seam allowances which can be let out if necessary.

attractive sturdy garments that wear well.

a selection of play clothes and everyday wear, with a few "best" items.

non-inflammable garments.

to have his or her feet measured every four months to ensure that shoes still fit.

drip-dry, crease-resistant garments which are colour-fast and pre-shrunk.

Here are some suitable fabrics to use when making clothes for babies and young children.

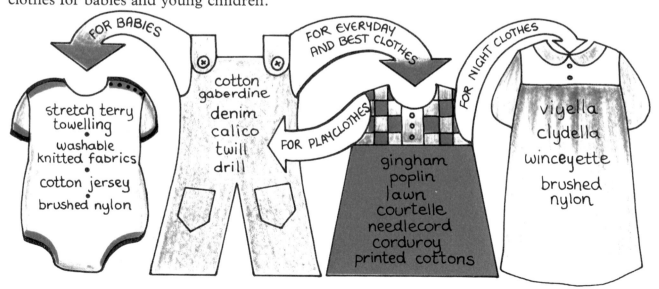

FOR BABIES
stretch terry towelling
washable knitted fabrics
cotton jersey
brushed nylon

FOR EVERYDAY AND BEST CLOTHES
cotton gaberdine
denim
calico
twill
drill

FOR PLAYCLOTHES
gingham
poplin
lawn
courtelle
needlecord
corduroy
printed cottons

FOR NIGHT CLOTHES
viyella
clydella
winceyette
brushed nylon

Think and Do

1. What are the advantages and disadvantages of buying clothes through a mail order firm?

2. Find out the current prices of:

a. a good-quality winter coat;

b. a well-cut skirt;

c. towelling nappies;

d. first size baby-stretch garments.

3. Imagine that you have been asked to advise an inexperienced dressmaker on what to buy and what to make when clothing her family. What would you say?

4. List the advantages and disadvantages of buying clothes at sales.

5. You are starting work and need new clothes. Choose four garments which you would buy or make. Briefly describe the colours, and show how you would mix them to make several outfits.

6. Look through magazines and find pictures of good basic styles which you would recommend for a teenager's wardrobe. Stick them neatly into your notebook under the headings:

a. clothes for work;

b. clothes for play;

c. clothes for special occasions.

7. Look through magazines and try to find an offer for a ready-to-sew garment. Say whether you like the style and fabric. Try to find a similar garment in a pattern book. From the details given, work out how much material would be needed. Price a suitable fabric and estimate the final cost of the finished garment. Compare the prices for the ready-to-sew garment and the similar garment made from your own fabric.

8. What advice would you give to a teenager starting work, who is anxious to dress well on a low budget?

9. Visit a local fashion boutique. Write a description of what you saw. List the advantages and disadvantages of buying clothes from this type of shop.

10. In your notebook, stick a suitable illustration or draw a picture of garments which you would recommend for each of the following:

a. a play overall or pop-over pinafore for a toddler;
b. a baby's sleep suit;
c. weatherproof protective clothing for a young schoolboy;
d. a christening outfit for a baby;
e. towelling beachwear for a 10-year-old girl.

Care of clothes

Clothes are expensive to buy so it is important to learn how to take good care of them. If you look after your wardrobe, keeping your clothes fresh and clean, you will always look smart and well dressed. Here are some general points to help you to prolong the life of your clothes.

1 After clothes have been worn they should be shaken or brushed before being hung in a wardrobe or folded neatly in a drawer. When clothes are hung correctly they shed their creases, and smell and feel fresher when next worn. Skirts hang best if they are suspended by the loops which are attached to the inside of the waistband. Multiple skirt and trouser hangers can be bought and these are useful when wardrobe space is limited. Do let clothes hang freely. Squashed clothes quickly become creased clothes. Garments which are placed in drawers should be folded properly. Underclothes and shirts have the folds ironed in, but outer garments should be folded loosely. When folding clothes, place sleeves towards the centre back, then fold across the length to form a square or oblong shape. Arrange collars and frills so that they lie neatly.

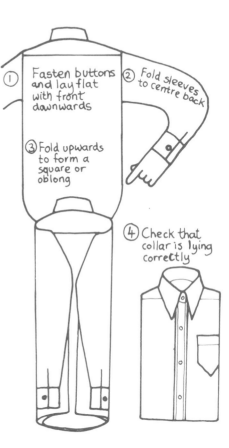

1. Fasten buttons and lay flat with front downwards
2. Fold sleeves to centre back
3. Fold upwards to form a square or oblong
4. Check that collar is lying correctly

2 Remove any stains from clothes immediately. This can often be done by rinsing the affected part of the garment in cold water, before the stain has had time to dry. If a stained garment washes well, then it may be left to soak in:

    a warm, soapy water;

    b warm water with an enzyme detergent.

Do *not* soak:

White cottons and linens may be left to soak in a cold, bleach solution.

    Most stains will be removed by either soaking the garment, or washing it at the maximum temperature suggested for that particular fabric. (See chart of wash care signs and symbols, page 48.) Obstinate stains can be treated with a special solvent or stain remover, but these should always be used with care. Do check that the fabric you are treating will not be harmed by the solvent.

    The chart overleaf shows some common stains and the special solvents needed for their removal.

    Stained garments which are not easy to wash can be dry cleaned. It is advisable to mention the nature of the stain when leaving a garment at the dry cleaner's.

3 Learn to use an iron correctly. Irons can be used for:

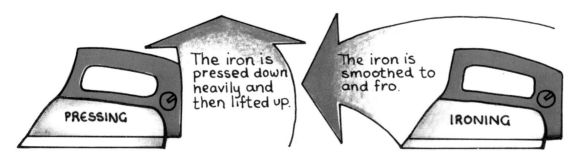

Stain	Treatment	Points to remember
Blood, egg and non-greasy food stains	Soak in cold water or use an enzyme washing powder. After treatment, rinse well or wash in the normal way.	
Grass	Use methylated spirits. After treatment, rinse well or wash in the normal way.	*Methylated spirits should not be used near a naked flame. It is INFLAMMABLE.*
Greasy food stains, oil and lipstick	Use carbon tetrachloride or a special grease solvent. After treatment, rinse well or wash in the normal way.	*Carbon tetrachloride should only be used in a well-ventilated room or in the open air. It has a poisonous vapour.*
Paint a oil-based	Use turpentine or a turpentine substitute. After treatment, rinse well or wash in the normal way.	*Paint stains must be removed immediately.*
b emulsion	Rinse in cold water or use methylated spirits.	
Nail varnish	Use acetone or a special nail varnish remover. After treatment, rinse well or wash in the normal way.	*Acetone is INFLAM-MABLE. Do not use near a naked flame. Always test a small piece of fabric with the solvent to check that there will be no damage.*
Coffee and tea	Soak in warm, soapy water or use an enzyme washing powder. For dried stains, rub with glycerine before soaking in a solution of sodium bicarbonate or borax. After treatment, rinse well or wash in the normal way.	

Stain	Treatment	Points to remember
Ink and iron mould	Soak in a solution of citric acid or lemon juice. After treatment, rinse well or wash in the normal way.	
Mildew and obstinate fruit stains	Soak in a solution of hypochlorite bleach. After treatment, rinse well or wash in the normal way.	*Only white fabrics can be treated in this way. Do not use on wool or silk.*
Chewing gum, bubbly gum and tar	Scrape off as much as possible. Soften the stain by rubbing with grease, e.g. lard, butter. Use carbon tetrachloride or a special grease solvent. After treatment, rinse well or wash in the normal way.	

The *International Textile Care Labelling Code* uses the symbol of an iron with a series of dots to denote the maximum temperature required for a fabric. Always refer to this label before ironing a garment.

When ironing, check to see which garments require a cool iron. Do these first. Then increase the temperature of the iron as needed. Always iron a damp garment until it is dry. Iron with long, sweeping movements, taking care not to iron a garment out of shape. When pressing, use a hot iron and always protect the fabric by placing a dampened pressing cloth between the garment and the iron. Pressing is used for opening seams and darts, flattening hems, giving a sharp edge to pleats and trousers, shaping gar-

	MACHINE	HAND WASH
4/50	Hand-hot medium wash	Hand-hot
	Cold rinse Short spin or drip-dry	
⬛	DO NOT USE CHLORINE BLEACH	
iron	WARM	
Ⓟ	DRY CLEANABLE	

HOT (210°C)   Cotton, linen, rayon or modified rayon.

 WARM (160°C) Polyester mixtures, wool.

 COOL (120°C) Acrylic, nylon, acetate, triacetate, polyester.

 DO NOT IRON.

ments, removing creases, shrinking fabrics and removing "shine" from woollens. Here are some points to help you when pressing.

a Garments are usually pressed on the wrong side but pleats and trousers are pressed on the right side.

b Adjust the pressure and heat of the iron to suit the weight of the fabric. Thin fabrics need little pressure, heavier fabrics require more pressure.

c Do not dampen the garment. Only dampen the pressing cloth.

d Press at each stage in dressmaking. Press hems and edges before stitching and seam turnings before neatening. Press darts, armhole seams, and openings.

e Skirt, coat, and dress seams should be pressed downwards.

f Napped fabrics should be pressed in the direction of the nap.

g Velvets, crêpes, and piled fabrics should be pressed with care. Stand an iron on its end and drape a damp cloth over the tip of the iron. Carefully draw the fabric over the iron, allowing the steam to penetrate the fabric.

h Use a cool iron when pressing synthetic fabrics.

i Always press a sample of the fabric before pressing the garment.

4 Check clothes frequently for any signs of general wear. Buttons should be sewn on firmly whenever they become loose, and tapes, seams, and hems will need regular attention. Loose stitching should be strengthened, and frayed buttonholes restitched. Any thin areas of material or small holes, can be darned to give extra life. When darning, use a long darning needle and a thread that will match the fabric.

To darn a thin place:

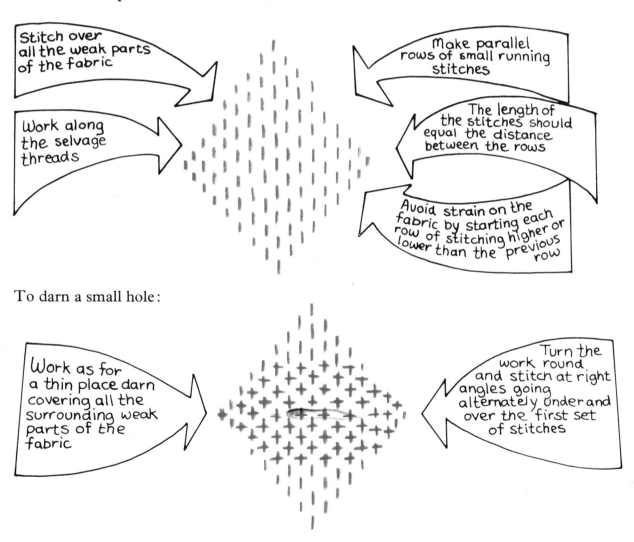

Stitch over all the weak parts of the fabric

Work along the selvage threads

Make parallel rows of small running stitches

The length of the stitches should equal the distance between the rows

Avoid strain on the fabric by starting each row of stitching higher or lower than the previous row

To darn a small hole:

Work as for a thin place darn covering all the surrounding weak parts of the fabric

Turn the work round and stitch at right angles going alternately under and over the first set of stitches

Most modern sewing machines can be used for darning. Machine darning gives a strong repair and is suitable for thin places, small holes and tears. When using a sewing machine for darning, read the instruction booklet carefully. You will need to:

    a attach a darning foot;

    b lower or cover the feed mechanism;

    c use an embroidery frame to hold the material firmly in position;

    d move the frame backwards and forwards under the needle to give neat, parallel rows of stitching across the area to be darned.

Small tears can often be mended by ironing or sticking a special tape over the slit on the wrong side of the material. It is also possible to camouflage holes by stitching or sticking bought patches and motifs over the affected area. This treatment is particularly useful when mending children's clothes.

Large holes in a garment will require patching. Patches should:

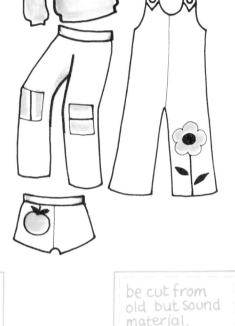

| match the garment in weave and colour | cover the hole and the weak area surrounding. | be cut from old but sound material. (New material will cause strain on the garment and may shrink) |

5 Remember that accessories are important too. Always keep stockings and gloves spotlessly clean. Handbags will need to be emptied occasionally and cosmetic purses checked. Shoes should be kept in a dust-free place when not being worn. Shoes which are worn regularly can be stacked in a special shoe tidy so that air can circulate around them. This helps to keep them fresh. Do remember that wet shoes should be dried out slowly. Do not place them in front of a roaring fire. Check frequently to see if shoes need mending. If they require attention, see to it

promptly. Always keep shoes clean. Leather shoes should be polished regularly and suede shoes should be brushed before being worn. A special suede polish can be used when necessary. Marks can be removed from vinyl shoes by wiping with a damp cloth. Obstinate stains may need to be rubbed gently with a little scouring powder.

However well you look after your clothes they will eventually become dirty and soiled. Loose dust can sometimes be removed by brushing, shaking, or beating, but engrained soiling requires different treatment. Clothes can be cleaned by:

sponging   **washing**   **dry cleaning**

Sponging   Sponging removes dirt, freshens colours, and helps to remove "shine" from a garment. This method of cleaning clothes is particularly suitable for heavy, bulky garments that are difficult to wash and dry, for example, suits, jackets, coats, thick dresses and skirts, and for those garments which are only slightly soiled. You will need: Work on a flat surface that has been covered with a thick towel.

- *a* Lay the garment flat.
- *b* With even strokes and working in one direction, sponge the garment clean. Heavily soiled areas may need to be rubbed gently.
- *c* Allow the garment to dry slightly.
- *d* **Press** with a hot iron. (Do not forget to use a pressing cloth.)
- *e* Air garment thoroughly.

a clean cloth or sponge

a basin containing a solution of warm water and 'soft' detergent

Washing   Today's range of machine-washable clothes has made home laundering processes much easier. Detailed washing instructions can usually be found on each garment, so a housewife need not be worried about how to wash an unfamiliar looking fabric. The wash care label will indicate how a garment should be machine or hand washed. The wash tub diagram consists of two figures:

This figure shows the wash process to be used

This figure gives the max. water temperature

Here is a complete chart of the wash care figures, signs and symbols which are now used on garments and household textiles.

White cotton and linen articles without special finishes

Cotton, linen or rayon articles without special finishes where colours are fast at 60°C

White nylon; white polyester/cotton mixtures .

Coloured nylon; polyester; cotton and rayon articles with special finishes; acrylic/cotton mixtures; coloured polyester/cotton mixtures

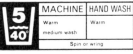
Cotton, linen or rayon articles where colours are fast at 40°C, but not at 60°C

Acrylics; acetate and triacetate, including mixtures with wool; polyester/wool blends

Wool, including blankets and wool mixtures with cotton or rayon; silk

Silk and printed acetate fabrics with colours not fast at 40°C

Cotton articles with special finishes capable of being boiled but requiring drip drying

Articles which must not be machine washed

Do not wash

A chlorine bleach can be used.

The temp. to set an iron is denoted by the number of dots.

Can be dry-cleaned. (The letters are instructions for the dry cleaners.)

Tumble dry

Line dry

Drip dry

Dry flat

If a wash care label shows any of the above signs crossed out, for example:

then these particular procedures should not be followed.

Remember that drip-dry garments should not be wrung or spun dry. They should be hung to dry in the same position in which they are worn.

Drip-dry garments look neater if creases are gently smoothed out while the clothes are drying. Pleats should be pulled into shape and collars, cuffs, and openings smoothed flat.

Dry cleaning   It is sometimes necessary to take a garment to be dry cleaned. This can be done at a laundry or at some laundrettes. The wash care label will indicate if dry cleaning is advisable. Dry cleaning can be expensive so it is worth considering this point when choosing clothing. Before leaving any garment to be dry cleaned, do:

   a check that all pockets are empty;
   b ask if any buttons, buckles, and belts should be removed;
   c indicate any stains that may require special attention.

Think and Do

1. What equipment is needed for pressing? Explain how you would press a pleated skirt.

2. Copy the diagram of the wash care labels (page 48) into your notebook.

3. Prepare a classroom display of trendy patches and motifs. See how many different kinds you can collect.

4. List the advantages and disadvantages of having clothes dry cleaned.

5. Say how you would sponge, press, and store a winter coat at the end of the season.

6. Find out the current price of:

a. a steam iron;

b. a card of grey darning wool;

c. a packet of "soft" detergent;

d. a card of iron-on tape for mending tears in children's trousers;

e. a packet of enzyme washing powder (E3 size);

f. a card of white shirt buttons;

g. a multiple skirt hanger;

h. a bottle of suede shoe cleaner.

7. Read the instruction booklet for an electric sewing machine carefully and find out how to darn. Work a small machine darn on a tray-cloth, tablecloth or pillow-case.

8. Say how you would:

a. repair a tear in the knee of some denim trousers;

b. remove a tea stain from a white cotton tablecloth;

c. dry a pair of wet shoes;

d. repair a thin place in the elbow of a woollen jumper.

9. You have been invited to attend for an interview. What special care would you give to your clothing and your person?

10. Copy the following sentences into your notebook. Say whether each one is *true* or *false.*

a. A fabric with a flame-resistant finish should not be soaked.

b. A symbol of an iron with one dot means that a hot iron can be used.

c. Napped fabrics should be pressed in the direction of the nap.

d. A drip-dry garment should be wrung well before being hung to dry.

e. Synthetic fabrics should be pressed with a cool iron.

f. An embroidery frame is used to hold material firmly in position during machine darning.

Part Two

About Fabrics

How fabrics are made

The last two decades have seen great advances in the textile industry. Today's fabrics can be produced in many different fibres and with a host of special finishes.

GINGHAM | POPLIN | DE[NIM] | SEERS[UCKER] | BROCADE | VELVET | GABERDINE | FLANNELETTE | TAFFETA

Some fibres, for example cotton, linen, wool, and silk, come from natural sources, but many fibres are man-made or manufactured—nylon, polyester, viscose rayon, acetate rayon, etc. Fabrics made from natural fibres have special qualities which make them cool to wear in summer and warm in winter. They will absorb sweat and so are comfortable and pleasant to the skin. Fabrics made from man-made fibres are often cheaper to buy than natural fabrics, and are hard-wearing and easy to clean. Some man-made fibres have the disadvantage of being non-absorbent and this makes them sticky and uncomfortable to wear in hot weather. Man-made fibres create static electricity and this readily attracts dirt. Fabrics can be made from a mixture or blend of natural and man-made fibres and these fabrics have the comfort of natural fibres combined with the toughness and easy-to-clean qualities of man-made fibres.

Fabrics are made by spinning fibres (hairs or fine threads) into yarn, or by collecting continuous filaments or fibres. These are then woven or knitted to produce cloth.

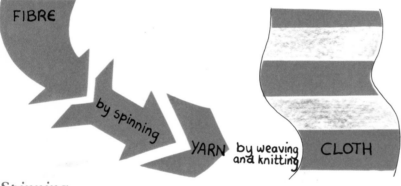

Spinning

Spinning was traditionally the work done by unmarried women, hence the name spinster. During the spinning process fibres are drawn and twisted together. Early man used to do this by hand. Then it was discovered that a fine thread could be spun by wrapping coarse wool around a distaff (stick) and pulling the wool thread out with a rotating spindle (a rounded rod of wood with pointed ends). A foot-operated spinning-wheel was then invented. During the eighteenth century there were great advances in the spinning industry. Water mills were used to power machinery, and inventions such as "the spinning jenny" (James Hargreaves) and "the spinning mule" (Samuel Crompton) helped to revolutionize the industry. A modern textile mill uses steam or electricity to drive massive and complicated spinning frames.

The spun yarn is woven or knitted into fabric.

Weaving

Weaving consists of crossing threads over and under each other, as in darning, on a piece of machinery called a loom. The warp threads run lengthways on the loom and the weft threads are interlaced backwards and forwards across them by means of a shuttle. The warp threads are fastened to a beam or roller at one end of the loom and the finished woven cloth is wrapped around another roller at the front. Two moveable frames (heddles or healds) are used to raise and lower alternate warp threads. Neatly finished edges, or selvages, form down the sides of the cloth.

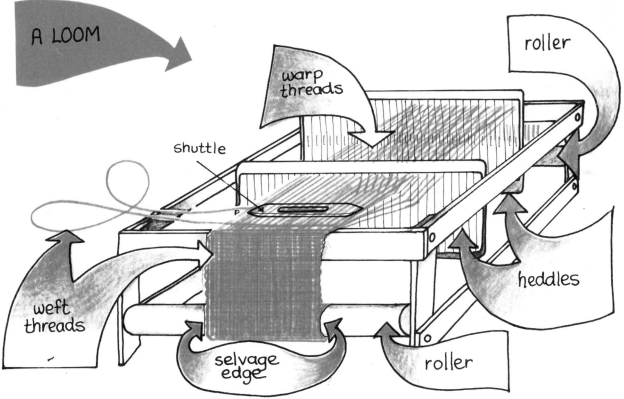

A LOOM

warp threads

roller

shuttle

weft threads

heddles

selvage edge

roller

The weaving of patterned fabrics is more difficult. Several shuttles each with a different-coloured thread may be used, and complicated patterns and intricate weaves can be formed.

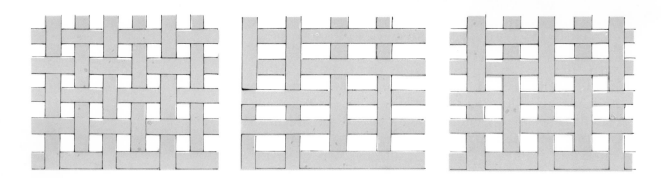

Sometimes different yarns are used for the warp and the weft threads, but the stronger yarn is always used for the warp threads.

After the weaving stage the fabric is "finished". This can involve several different processes which give shine, colour, and special surface finishes to the cloth. We will learn more about these special finishes in Chapter 9.

Knitting

In addition to weaving, fabrics can also be produced by knitting yarns together. The process is similar to hand knitting and consists of joining threads by means of loops. Complicated machinery is used to produce today's knitted fabrics and most fibres are suitable for this type of fabric production. Because of their loop structure, knitted fabrics will stretch. Special frames can be used to produce tubular knitted cloth.

Felting

This is a process by which fibres are matted or bonded together under heat and pressure. It produces a fabric without grain, which can be cut in any direction, and which will not unravel. This process is used in the making of non-woven interfacings and interlinings, and in the production of felt.

Bonding

In this process two fabrics are stuck or bonded together. A

special foam is used as an adhesive, and this gives extra bulk to the bonded fabric, making it heavier and warmer to wear.

Knotting

There are several ways of making fabric from yarn by using knots. Crocheting, tatting, and macramé are the methods most commonly used.

Giving colour to fabrics

Colour can be added to fabrics by:

using coloured yarn

dyeing the cloth after it has been woven

printing a design on the surface of the fabric

Early man added colour to his clothes by using the juices from berries, plants, animals, and insects as dyes. Today's dyes are manufactured from chemicals obtained from coal tar. Dyeing takes place in large containers or vats in which the yarn or cloth is soaked. Each type of fibre requires a special dye. Some fibres are difficult to dye and a special chemical called a mordant has to be used to fix the dye in the fibre.

When a pattern or design is being printed on fabric, the cloth passes under revolving copper cylinders. These cylinders are engraved with the required pattern and contain the dye to be used. As the cloth passes under the cylinders, the coloured design is transferred on to the surface of the cloth.

Fabrics can also be screen printed or block printed, but these processes are expensive.

Think and Do

1. Draw and colour a design suitable for a hand-printed head square.

2. Prepare a class display on yarns. See how many different colours, thicknesses, and types you can collect.

3. Visit your school and local libraries and find out all you can on:

a. the spinning jenny;

b. the spinning mule;

c. a modern weaving loom;

d. a modern dyeworks.

4. Cut out samples of:

a. a woven fabric;

b. a knitted fabric;

c. a felted fabric.

Stick them into your notebook and in your own words say how each one was made.

5. Copy the diagram of a weaving loom (page 57) into your notebook. Label the following parts clearly: warp and weft threads; selvages; heddles; shuttle; rollers.

6. Choose a word from Column B to complete each sentence in Column A. Write out the completed sentences.

Column A	*Column B*
a. ...... fibres absorb sweat.	*weft*
b. Weaving is done on a	*spindle*
c. In olden days thread was spun by using a distaff and	*natural*
d. ...... fibres create static electricity.	*mordant*
e. A ...... is a chemical which helps to fix and stabilize dyes.	*man-made*
f. The ...... threads run lengthways when weaving.	*loom*
g. The ...... threads are contained in the shuttle.	*heddle*
h. The ...... is a frame which raises and lowers the warp thread.	*warp*

7. Weave some simple patterns. Use flattened drinking straws, narrow strips of paper, raffia, or cane for the warp and weft threads.

8. In 1856 a man called William Perkin made a discovery which revolutionized the dyeing of fabrics. Try to find out what he discovered and why his discovery was so important.

9. Copy out this crossword and complete it.

Clues across

1. This process produces a fabric without grain.
2. A fabric made by tying yarn into knots.
3. The inventor of the spinning mule.
4. This side edge of fabric will not unravel.

Clues down

5. In the eighteenth century this was used to power machines in the textile industry.
6. Knitted fabrics will do this.
7. Made by spinning fibres.
8. This is used when bonding two fabrics together.

10. Visit the fabric department of a large store and look at a selection of woven fabrics. Notice how different weaves can produce different patterned effects on the surface of the fabric. Find out the names of some common weaves.

Natural fibres

Natural fibres are obtained from animals and plants. Wool, silk, cotton, and linen are the most important.

Wool

Wool is an animal fibre. It is obtained mainly from the fleece of sheep but other animal fibres can be used. Alpaca, cashmere, and mohair are wool fibres which come from different breeds of goat, and angora is obtained from the angora rabbit. The hair of camels and llama can also be used to produce wool.

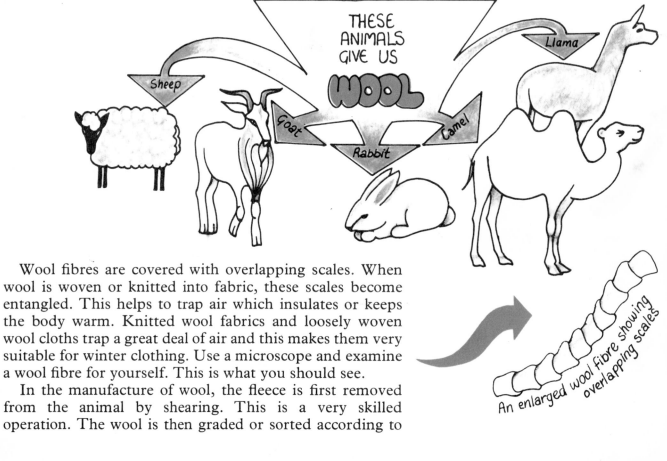

THESE ANIMALS GIVE US WOOL

Sheep · Goat · Rabbit · Camel · Llama

An enlarged wool fibre showing overlapping scales

Wool fibres are covered with overlapping scales. When wool is woven or knitted into fabric, these scales become entangled. This helps to trap air which insulates or keeps the body warm. Knitted wool fabrics and loosely woven wool cloths trap a great deal of air and this makes them very suitable for winter clothing. Use a microscope and examine a wool fibre for yourself. This is what you should see.

In the manufacture of wool, the fleece is first removed from the animal by shearing. This is a very skilled operation. The wool is then graded or sorted according to its quality, and sent to woollen mills. Untreated wool is tangled and very dirty, and contains animal grease. At the mill the fleece is cleaned thoroughly. The wool fibres are brushed or carded, and then combed and drawn out. Long wool fibres are spun on a frame and woven on a loom to make worsted material. Short wool fibres are turned into woollen yarn, in which the fibres are mixed together instead of lying parallel as in worsted. The woollen yarn is spun and then woven to give a soft cloth with a fluffy surface. Very short wool fibres cannot be spun and these are shrunk and pressed together to make felt.

Wool can be dyed at the yarn stage or when it has been woven into cloth.

Here are the main advantages and disadvantages of woollen fabrics.

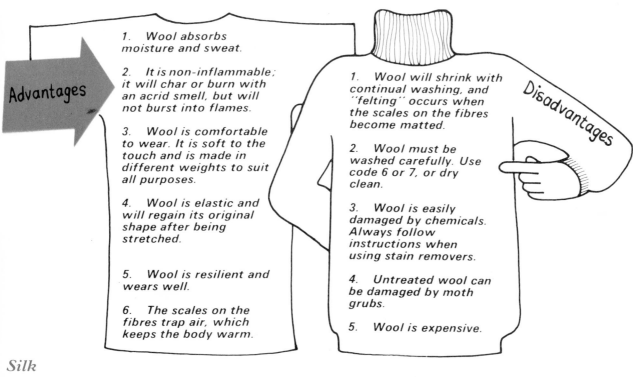

Advantages

1. Wool absorbs moisture and sweat.

2. It is non-inflammable; it will char or burn with an acrid smell, but will not burst into flames.

3. Wool is comfortable to wear. It is soft to the touch and is made in different weights to suit all purposes.

4. Wool is elastic and will regain its original shape after being stretched.

5. Wool is resilient and wears well.

6. The scales on the fibres trap air, which keeps the body warm.

Disadvantages

1. Wool will shrink with continual washing, and "felting" occurs when the scales on the fibres become matted.

2. Wool must be washed carefully. Use code 6 or 7, or dry clean.

3. Wool is easily damaged by chemicals. Always follow instructions when using stain removers.

4. Untreated wool can be damaged by moth grubs.

5. Wool is expensive.

Silk

Silk is an animal fibre which is produced by the silkworm.

The silkworm feeds on chopped-up mulberry leaves and grows rapidly in size, until it is ready to change into a

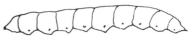

chrysalis. It then spins an egg-shaped cocoon around itself by producing a sticky liquid which hardens into a silken thread. The caterpillar winds this long silken filament round and round itself until the cocoon is complete.

During the manufacture of silk the grubs are destroyed. If moths were allowed to develop they would break through the cocoon and damage the silk filament. The cocoons are placed in boiling water to soften the gum. The threads of silk are drawn off and wound around a frame. It is possible to unwind about one quarter of the silk from a cocoon in an unbroken filament. This type of silk is very fine and is known as thrown or raw silk. The threads may be twisted to add strength before being wound into skeins. When the silk filaments break, the rest of the silk is made into spun silk. The short lengths are combed, drawn out, and spun to produce silken yarn. Both thrown and spun silk can be woven on looms or knitted.

Here are the main advantages and disadvantages of silk fabrics.

Advantages

1.   Silk is a very strong thread and silk fabrics wear well.

2.   Silk is absorbent and will soak up moisture and sweat.

3.   Silk is warm to wear. It is a bad conductor of heat and therefore traps body warmth.

4.   It is light to wear, soft to the touch, and drapes well.

5.   Silk is elastic and keeps its shape well.

6.   Silk has an attractive sheen or lustre.

7.   Silk will dye easily.

8.   Silk is non-inflammable. It will melt slowly and has an acrid smell but does not burst into flames.

Disadvantages

1.   Silk is damaged by heat. Care must be taken when washing. Use code 7 or dry clean.

2.   Silk is damaged by chemicals. Be careful with stain removers and avoid alkalis.

3.   Silk is expensive.

4.   Silk is easily damaged by the salt content of perspiration.

Cotton

Cotton is a vegetable fibre which comes from the cotton plant. The cotton plant flourishes in a warm climate but needs a wet soil. Today, cotton is grown in Asia, America, India, China, Egypt, and many countries in Africa. The finest type of cotton is "Sea Island cotton", which has long fibres and is grown in the West Indies.

The cotton plant has a round, fluffy seed pod which is called a bol.

When the seeds are ripe, the bol bursts and the cotton wool fibres are gathered. The fibres are then separated from seeds, stalks, and leaves by a process called ginning, which drags the cotton fibres through narrow slots. The cotton fibres are then packed tightly into bales and transported to cotton mills. At the mills the bales of cotton fibres are broken open and the fibres are pulled, brushed, drawn out, and carded by complicated machinery, until a fine sliver is produced which can be twisted and then spun into yarn. Cotton can be woven or knitted. It is usually bleached before being dyed or printed.

Here are the main advantages and disadvantages of cotton fabrics.

The fluffy seed pod or bol of the cotton plant

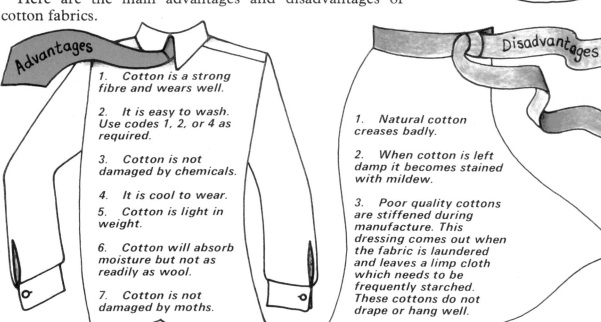

Advantages

1. Cotton is a strong fibre and wears well.

2. It is easy to wash. Use codes 1, 2, or 4 as required.

3. Cotton is not damaged by chemicals.

4. It is cool to wear.

5. Cotton is light in weight.

6. Cotton will absorb moisture but not as readily as wool.

7. Cotton is not damaged by moths.

Disadvantages

1. Natural cotton creases badly.

2. When cotton is left damp it becomes stained with mildew.

3. Poor quality cottons are stiffened during manufacture. This dressing comes out when the fabric is laundered and leaves a limp cloth which needs to be frequently starched. These cottons do not drape or hang well.

Linen

Linen is a vegetable fibre which comes from the stalks of the flax plant. Flax grows in many parts of the world, but Belgium and Ireland are particularly famous for the manufacture of linen. Flax is an annual plant which bears bright blue or red flowers and has a long stalk.

Bundles of fibres run lengthways down the stalk of the plant. When the flax is ready to be harvested, the long stalks are taken to the linen mill where they are thoroughly cleaned and combed. This is necessary to remove any seeds, leaves, and dirt. Then the stalks are soaked in water. During this stage the gum binding the fibres together is softened. This process is called retting. The loosened fibres are then dried by hot air. The woody parts of the stalks are broken up and removed by machinery, leaving the linen fibres which are then drawn out ready for spinning. Linen is woven on looms. Intricate patterns can be made, as in damask cloths. Linen is usually bleached and this can be done either naturally, using the action of the sun and rain, or by chemicals.

Here are the main advantages and disadvantages of linen fabrics.

The flax plant

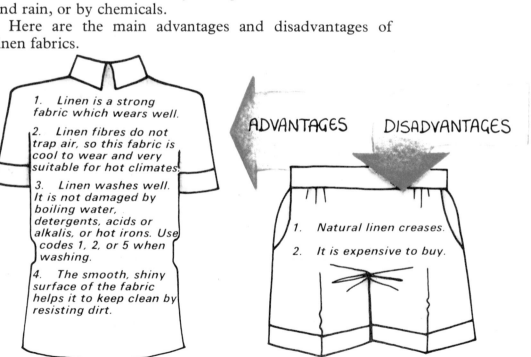

ADVANTAGES

1. Linen is a strong fabric which wears well.

2. Linen fibres do not trap air, so this fabric is cool to wear and very suitable for hot climates.

3. Linen washes well. It is not damaged by boiling water, detergents, acids or alkalis, or hot irons. Use codes 1, 2, or 5 when washing.

4. The smooth, shiny surface of the fabric helps it to keep clean by resisting dirt.

DISADVANTAGES

1. Natural linen creases.

2. It is expensive to buy.

Other vegetable fibres

Jute is a tropical plant. Its stalk is used for making sack-cloth, hessian, ropes, and carpets. Hemp is used to make canvas and rope. The fibrous outer husk of the coconut can be spun into a yarn which is then made into coconut matting. Maize fibres can be used for matting, and sisal is spun and woven into rugs. Several other strong grasses are spun and woven into material.

Each natural fibre has its own individual advantages and disadvantages but to help you when choosing and using natural fibres, here are the main points to remember:

a   most natural fibres are soft and comfortable to wear;

b   most are absorbent;

c   they are easy to handle and sew;

d   some are warm to wear, e.g. wool, silk, and some are cool, e.g. cotton, linen;

e   they are attractive fibres which have a pleasing appearance;

f   unless they have been treated with special finishes, they can shrink, felt, or fray when laundered;

g   blends of natural and man-made fibres produce fabrics which have the comfort, softness, and absorbency of natural fibres, combined with the hard-wearing properties of man-made fibres.

Think and Do

1. Are these sentences *true* or *false?*
a. Silk is an animal fibre.
b. Angora is a soft wool which is obtained from the angora camel.
c. Spun silk is made from the shorter, broken lengths of silk filament.
d. The round seed pod of the cotton plant is called a pol.
e. Cotton can be damaged by moths.

f. Linen is a cheap fabric to buy.

g. Wool is very absorbent.

h. The silkworm feeds on mulberry leaves.

2. What is meant by each of the following terms:

a. retting;

b. ginning;

c. raw silk;

d. worsted?

3. Copy the following diagram into your notebook and write a descriptive sentence in each of the boxes.

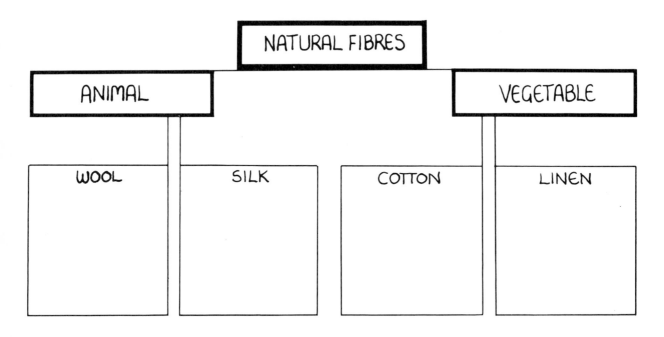

4. Say how you would launder each of the following:

a. an apron made of poor-quality cotton;

b. a woollen cardigan;

c. a linen tablecloth;

d. a pair of cotton pyjamas.

5. Make a list of the various stages in the manufacture of woollen cloth.

6. Using an atlas or globe find the main cotton and flax growing areas of the world.

7. Complete the following sentences using the correct word from the alternatives given in the brackets:

a. Worsted material is made from *(short, long)* wool fibres.

b. Unbroken lengths of silk filament are called *(thrown, drawn)* silk.

c. Coconut matting is made from the *(seed, outer husk)* of the coconut.

d. Wool fibres are covered with overlapping *(spots, scales)*.

e. Sea Island cotton is grown in the *(Mediterranean, West Indies)*.

f. Linen is a vegetable fibre which comes from the stalks of the *(flax, hemp)* plant.

8. Collect small pieces of wool, silk, cotton, and linen fabrics. Burn each piece separately. Write a description in your notebook of what you saw and smelled. Do use an evaporating dish or ovenproof plate when trying this experiment and BE CAREFUL.

9. Use your school and local libraries to find out all you can on:

a. the life cycle of a silk-spinning moth;

b. the Woolsack;

c. slave labour in the cotton plantations of America.

10. Suggest a natural fabric which you think would be suitable for each of the following garments. Give reasons for your choice.

a. an underskirt;

b. a summer dress;

c. a winter suit;

d. a nightdress;

e. a shawl;

f. a tennis outfit;

g. a baby's vest;

h. a long leisure- or evening-dress.

Man-made fibres

Man-made fibres can be manufactured from natural products, for example wood, milk, peanuts, seaweed, soya beans, and maize, or they can be made entirely from chemical substances such as coal tar and oil. Fibres which are made from natural products are called regenerated fibres, and completely artificial fibres are called synthetic fibres.

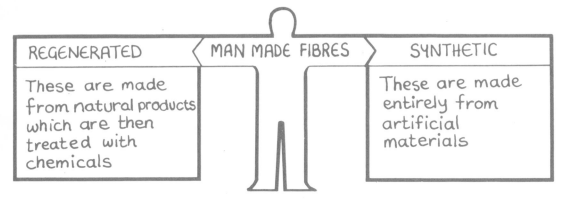

REGENERATED   MAN MADE FIBRES   SYNTHETIC

These are made from natural products which are then treated with chemicals

These are made entirely from artificial materials

There are many different types of man-made fibres.

Rayon

Rayon is made from cellulose which is the fleshy part of wood and plants. There are two main types of rayon — viscose and acetate.

Viscose rayon is made from bleached wood pulp which has been broken down and pressed into thin sheets. The sheets of wood pulp are steeped in a caustic soda solution and then treated with a chemical called carbon bi-sulphide. The dissolved cellulose forms a syrup-like liquid called viscose, which is orange in colour. The viscose is forced through tiny holes in spinnerets to form fine filaments of rayon which are then hardened in a bath of sulphuric acid. The filaments or threads are washed, bleached, and twisted together to form yarn. Viscose rayon can then be woven or knitted.

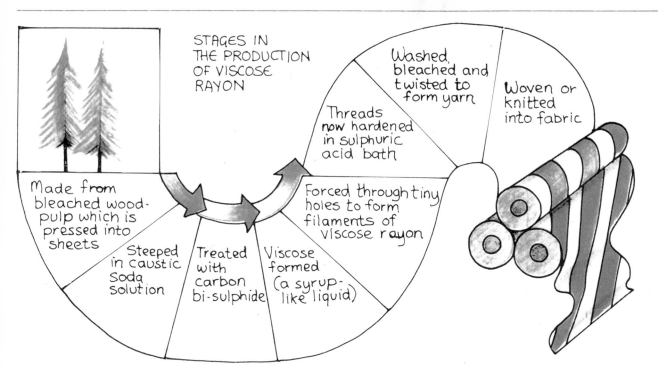

STAGES IN THE PRODUCTION OF VISCOSE RAYON

Made from bleached wood-pulp which is pressed into sheets

Steeped in caustic soda solution

Treated with carbon bi-sulphide

Viscose formed (a syrup-like liquid)

Forced through tiny holes to form filaments of viscose rayon

Threads now hardened in sulphuric acid bath

Washed, bleached and twisted to form yarn

Woven or knitted into fabric

Here are the main advantages and disadvantages of viscose rayon fabrics.

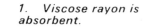

Advantages

1. *Viscose rayon is absorbent.*

2. *It drapes well.*

3. *It resembles silk but is much cheaper to buy.*

4. *Viscose rayon is sometimes given a brushed finish and used as a cheap substitute for wool.*

5. *It can be blended with other fibres—for example, wool or cotton.*

6. *Viscose rayon does not shrink.*

1. *Viscose rayon is weakened by water. Always read washing instructions carefully. Treatment will vary according to the mixture of fibres in the fabric.*

2. *It is damaged by strong chemicals.*

Disadvantages

Acetate rayon is made from cotton linters, which are the short fibres discarded during the ginning of cotton. The cotton linters are first dissolved in acetic acid and acetic anhydride. The solution is then heated and flakes of acetate rayon are formed. These are dissolved in acetone to form a thick liquid. The liquid acetate rayon is forced through tiny holes and forms continuous filaments which solidify in warm air. The filaments are twisted to form yarn and then woven or knitted into fabric.

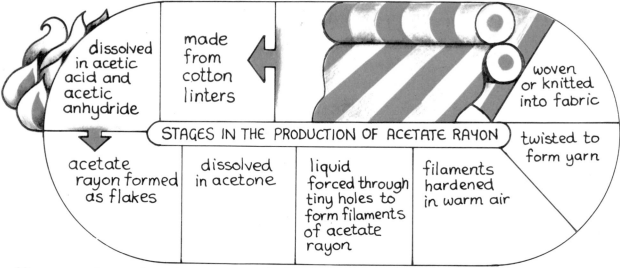

STAGES IN THE PRODUCTION OF ACETATE RAYON

- made from cotton linters
- dissolved in acetic acid and acetic anhydride
- acetate rayon formed as flakes
- dissolved in acetone
- liquid forced through tiny holes to form filaments of acetate rayon
- filaments hardened in warm air
- twisted to form yarn
- woven or knitted into fabric

Here are the main advantages and disadvantages of acetate rayon fabrics.

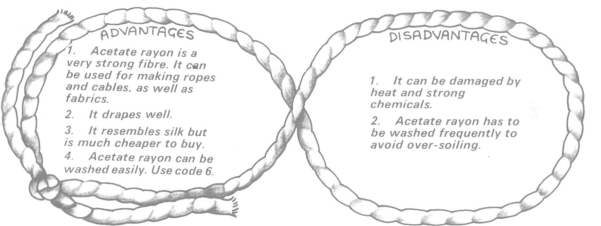

ADVANTAGES

1. Acetate rayon is a very strong fibre. It can be used for making ropes and cables, as well as fabrics.

2. It drapes well.

3. It resembles silk but is much cheaper to buy.

4. Acetate rayon can be washed easily. Use code 6.

DISADVANTAGES

1. It can be damaged by heat and strong chemicals.

2. Acetate rayon has to be washed frequently to avoid over-soiling.

Triacetate is a variation of acetate rayon and is made from wood pulp and cotton linters. It has a silky, shiny finish and is a crease-resistant fabric. It can be permanently pleated and is very easy to launder. Use codes 6 or 8.

Rayon can be produced as:

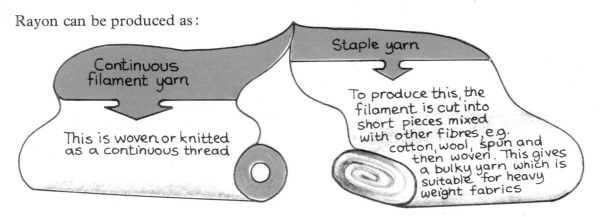

Continuous filament yarn

This is woven or knitted as a continuous thread

Staple yarn

To produce this, the filament is cut into short pieces mixed with other fibres, e.g. cotton, wool, spun and then woven. This gives a bulky yarn which is suitable for heavy weight fabrics

Rayon fibres can be spun, woven, and finished to make many different fabrics. Here are a few examples.

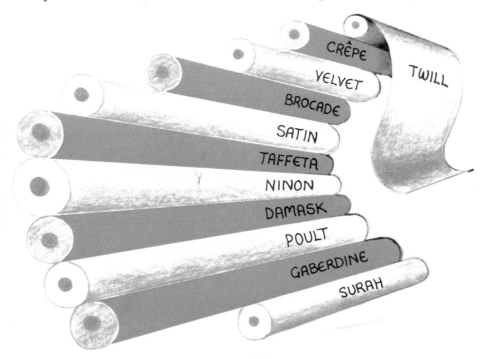

CRÊPE
VELVET
BROCADE
SATIN
TAFFETA
NINON
DAMASK
POULT
GABERDINE
SURAH
TWILL

Protein fibres

Man-made fibres can be manufactured from protein, which is obtained from various animal and vegetable sources. The main sources are:

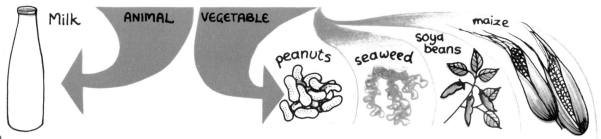

Protein fibres, such as Fibrolane and Aralac, are suitable for underwear and nightwear, and are used in the manufacture of blankets and carpets.

Here are the main advantages and disadvantages of protein fabrics.

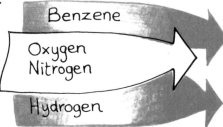

ADVANTAGES
1. Protein fibres are soft, warm, and absorbent.

2. They resemble wool.

DISADVANTAGE
Protein fibres are weak. Their strength is improved when they are blended with stronger fibres—for example, wool, rayon, nylon, and cotton.

Nylon

Nylon is a synthetic or completely artificial fibre which is manufactured from:

Benzene — obtained from coal

Oxygen Nitrogen — from air

Hydrogen — from water

Nylon is a relatively new fibre. It was invented by an American scientist called Carruthers, in 1930. The manufacture of nylon yarn is very complicated. Two chemicals (adipic acid and hexamethylene diamine) are dissolved in alcohol. They are then mixed with nitrogen gas to form a nylon salt. This is dissolved in water and heated. The liquid nylon is forced through a spinneret and forms a continuous filament when cooled. The filament is stretched to increase its strength and elasticity, and then twisted to give nylon yarn. This can be woven or knitted into fabric.

Another method of producing nylon fabric is to make a thick ribbon of nylon, which is then broken into tiny pieces or polymer chips. The chips are melted to give a sticky liquid which is then forced through spinnerets. The filaments are cut into short pieces and spun to make staple fibres. These are then woven or knitted.

Here are the main advantages and disadvantages of nylon fabrics.

ADVANTAGES

1. It is very strong.

2. Nylon is light in weight and has a fine silk-like appearance.

3. It is elastic. This makes it suitable for stockings and tights.

4. Most nylons are non inflammable and melt into a black bead-like substance.

5. Nylon is crease-resistant and very easy to launder. Use codes 3 or 4.

6. It can be blended with other fibres.

7. It is mothproof and cannot be damaged by rubbing and abrasive action, or by mildew.

8. Nylon can be heat-set to give permanent pleating.

DISADVANTAGES

1. Nylon is not absorbent and this can make nylon underwear and nightwear uncomfortable to the skin.

2. Nylon is easily soiled because of the static electricity created.

3. It can be damaged by some acids, bleaching agents, and strong sunlight.

4. Nylon frays badly. Use pinking shears after cutting out, and make french seams whenever possible.

Polyester

Terylene was the first polyester fibre to be invented. Polyesters are made from two chemicals, ethylene glycol and terephthalic acid, which are obtained from petroleum. The manufacturing processes are similar to that of nylon. Polyester fibres can be used as continuous filaments or staple fibres, and can be woven or knitted into fabrics.

Here are the main advantages and disadvantages of polyester fabrics.

ADVANTAGES

1. Polyester is a very strong fabric which is not weakened when wet.

2. It is a soft fabric which drapes well.

3. Polyester is not damaged by sunlight.

4. It does not shrink.

5. It is crease-resistant.

6. Polyester is elastic but not as much as nylon.

7. It is very easy to launder. Use code 4.

8. Polyester can be heat-set to give permanent pleating.

9. It is not damaged by moths, mildew, acids, alkalis, or bleaches.

10. Polyester can be blended with other fibres, for example, wool or cotton.

DISADVANTAGES

1. Polyester is not very absorbent.

2. Some polyesters slip during sewing. Terylene will fray.

Acrylic

Acrylic fibres are made from the liquid chemical acrylonitrile. Acrylic fibres can be woven or knitted as staple yarn into many different kinds of fabric.

Here are the main advantages and disadvantages of acrylic fabrics.

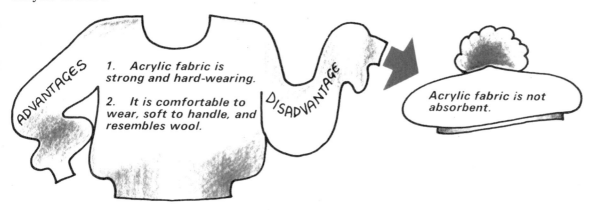

ADVANTAGES

1. Acrylic fabric is strong and hard-wearing.

2. It is comfortable to wear, soft to handle, and resembles wool.

DISADVANTAGE

Acrylic fabric is not absorbent.

Man-made fibres are sold under various trade names. Here are some of them.

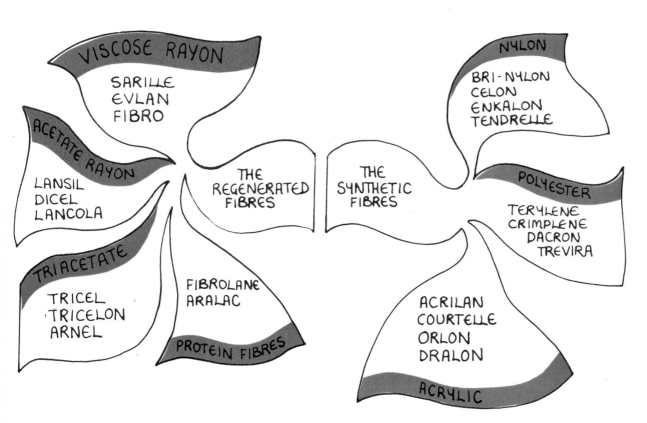

VISCOSE RAYON
SARILLE
EVLAN
FIBRO

NYLON
BRI-NYLON
CELON
ENKALON
TENDRELLE

ACETATE RAYON
LANSIL
DICEL
LANCOLA

THE REGENERATED FIBRES

THE SYNTHETIC FIBRES

POLYESTER
TERYLENE
CRIMPLENE
DACRON
TREVIRA

TRIACETATE
TRICEL
TRICELON
ARNEL

FIBROLANE
ARALAC
PROTEIN FIBRES

ACRILAN
COURTELLE
ORLON
DRALON
ACRYLIC

Each man-made fibre has its own individual advantages and disadvantages, but to help you when choosing and using man-made fibres, here are the main general points to remember:

 a they are strong and hard-wearing;
 b they can be laundered easily, and will drip dry;
 c bulked yarns give added warmth, elasticity, and absorbency;
 d some fray easily;
 e some attract dirt readily;
 f blends of man-made and natural fibres produce fabrics which have the hard-wearing properties of man-made fibres, combined with the comfort, softness, and absorbency of natural fibres.

Synthetic fibres can also be made from glass, asbestos, and metals such as gold and silver. Glass fibres can be woven into a fabric which is used for curtains and other soft furnishings. Asbestos fibres are used in the making of protective fire-proof clothing, and metallic threads can be used to add sparkle and decoration to most types of fabric.

Think and Do

1. Design a poster to promote an entirely new man-made fabric. Give your fabric a name and stress its many advantages and uses.

2. Re-arrange these letters to give well-known trade names for man-made fabrics.

a. IALCNRA   *e.* ETNLEEYR
b. LONRO   *f.* IMLCEERPN
c. YNOLN   *g.* LORDNA
d. ICTLER   *h.* ONEBLAFIR

3. In your own words describe the various stages in the manufacture of nylon or viscose rayon. Use charts or diagrams where possible.

4. Say what is meant by the following terms:

a. viscose;

b. protein fibre;

c. staple yarn;

d. polymer chips.

5. Prepare a class display on man-made fabrics. See how many different kinds of material you can collect.

6. Imagine that you are making a summer dress. In your notebook, sketch a suitable style. Underneath, indicate which man-made fabric you would choose for the dress and give reasons for your choice.

7. Cut out samples of regenerated and synthetic fabrics. Stick them neatly into your notebook and underneath each one describe:

a. the fibre from which it is made;

b. the way it should be laundered.

8. Polyester/cotton fabric is suitable for a variety of garments.

a. Make a list of garments which you could buy or make from polyester/cotton fabric.

b. Suggest other man-made/natural fibre blends and their uses.

9. Write the following sentences into your notebook using the correct word from the words in the brackets.

a. Acetate rayon is made from *(coal tar, cotton linters).*

b. Crimplene belongs to the *(nylon, polyester)* group of man-made fibres.

c. Filaments of viscose rayon are hardened in a bath of *(sulphuric acid, acetone),* before being woven or knitted into fabric.

d. Protein fibres are *(soft, hard)* fibres which resemble *(cotton, wool).*

e. (Terylene, Trevira) was the first polyester fabric to be manufactured.

f. Fibres made from protein belong to the *(synthetic, regenerated)* group of man-made fibres.

10. Copy out this crossword and complete it.

Clues across

1. A type of rayon.
2. A polyester fibre.
3. This group of man-made fibres is manufactured from artificial materials.

Clues down

4. This fibre is made from acrylonitrile.
5. One of the products used in the making of nylon.
6. This vegetable provides protein which can be used to make fibres.

Fabric finishes

Fabrics can be produced from a variety of different weaving or knitting patterns. The weave or knit used affects the final appearance of the fabric. For example, twill fabrics are woven (sometimes knitted) with a characteristic diagonal line running along the face of the cloth, and it is this which gives the fabric its name. The actual fibre used does not normally affect the name of the fabric. This is decided by:

the weave or knit and **the appearance of the finished fabric**

Opposite are descriptions of the weave/knit and appearance of some well-known fabrics. How many would you be able to recognize?

Scientists are continually trying to find new ways of improving fabrics by giving them special finishes. These special treatments can either enhance the appearance of a fabric or reduce the disadvantages of any particular fibre. For example, wool will shrink when washed frequently, but woollen fabrics can now be given a shrink-resistant finish that prevents this happening. Look at page 83 to see how fabrics can be treated.

It used to be necessary to wash certain "weak" fabrics by hand, but today most materials can be machine-washed. This is a great help to the busy housewife who has only to check with the wash care label on the fabric to discover the machine- or hand-washing procedures necessary. Many garments now have a drip-dry and minimum-iron finish, making home-laundering processes easier.

The loop structure of knitted fabrics has always given them an elastic quality. It is now possible to produce woven fabrics that will stretch in a similar way. This is done by bulking the yarn, a process that fluffs the fibres to give elasticity and absorbency. Bulked yarns are often

FABRICS WITH A "WOOLLEN" APPEARANCE

SERGE A hard-wearing, rather wiry fabric which has a twill weave.

GABERDINE A tightly woven fabric with a diagonal twill weave.

BARATHEA A fabric with a close twill and a characteristic "pebble" finish.

TWILL A fabric with a diagonal weave on the face of the cloth.

BOUCLÉ A curly-looking fabric which is woven or knitted with looped yarn.

FLANNEL A soft fabric that has a napped surface. Can have a plain or twill weave.

VELOUR A fabric with a short, thick pile. Can have a plain or satin weave.

FABRICS WITH A "SILKEN" APPEARANCE

SATIN A smooth fabric which has a shiny finish.

VELVET A smooth fabric with a thick cut pile.

BROCADE A satin fabric with a rich, pronounced pattern or design.

CHIFFON A light and delicate fabric with a plain weave.

GROSGRAIN A closely woven fabric with a fine horizontal rib.

TAFFETA A plain, woven fabric that has a crisp feel.

TUSSORE A fabric with an uneven surface and texture.

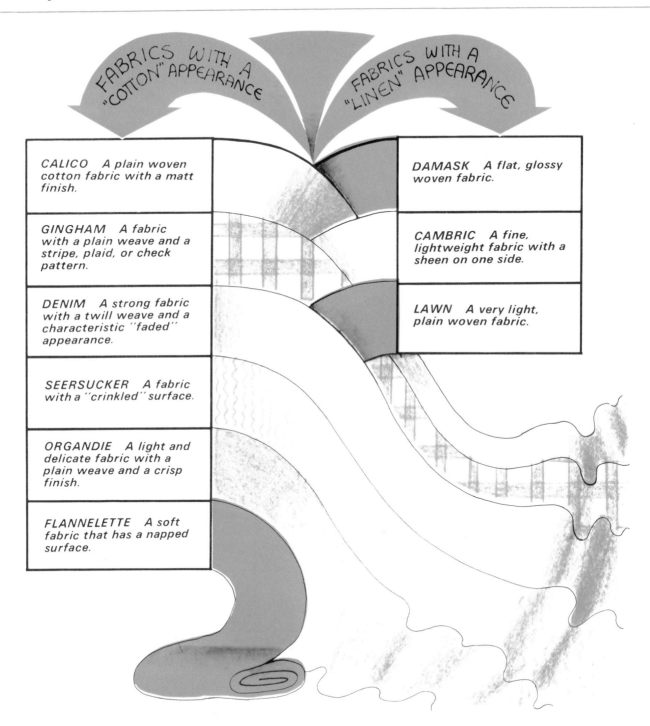

FABRICS WITH A "COTTON" APPEARANCE

FABRICS WITH A "LINEN" APPEARANCE

CALICO   A plain woven cotton fabric with a matt finish.

DAMASK   A flat, glossy woven fabric.

GINGHAM   A fabric with a plain weave and a stripe, plaid, or check pattern.

CAMBRIC   A fine, lightweight fabric with a sheen on one side.

DENIM   A strong fabric with a twill weave and a characteristic "faded" appearance.

LAWN   A very light, plain woven fabric.

SEERSUCKER   A fabric with a "crinkled" surface.

ORGANDIE   A light and delicate fabric with a plain weave and a crisp finish.

FLANNELETTE   A soft fabric that has a napped surface.

mixed with elastomeric stretch yarns (for example, Lycra, Spanzelle), to make foundation garments, babies' stretch clothing, and swimsuits.

Fabrics can be treated to make them:

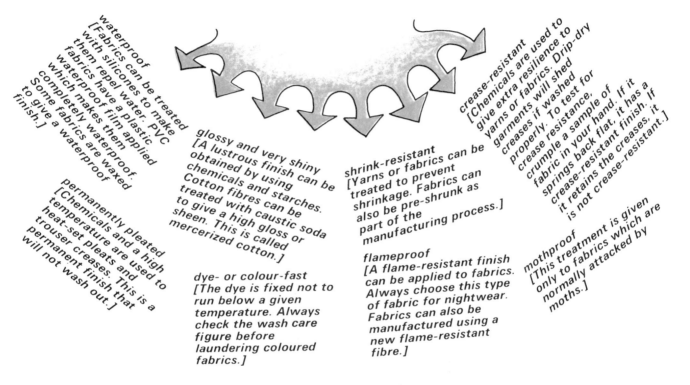

waterproof
[Fabrics can be treated with silicones to make them repel water. PVC fabrics have a plastic waterproof film applied which makes them completely waterproof. Some fabrics are waxed to give a waterproof finish.]

glossy and very shiny
[A lustrous finish can be obtained by using chemicals and starches. Cotton fibres can be treated with caustic soda to give a high gloss or sheen. This is called mercerized cotton.]

permanently pleated
[Chemicals and a high temperature are used to heat-set pleats and trouser creases. This is a permanent finish that will not wash out.]

dye- or colour-fast
[The dye is fixed not to run below a given temperature. Always check the wash care figure before laundering coloured fabrics.]

shrink-resistant
[Yarns or fabrics can be treated to prevent shrinkage. Fabrics can also be pre-shrunk as part of the manufacturing process.]

flameproof
[A flame-resistant finish can be applied to fabrics. Always choose this type of fabric for nightwear. Fabrics can also be manufactured using a new flame-resistant fibre.]

crease-resistant
[Chemicals are used to give extra resilience to yarns or fabrics. Drip-dry garments will shed creases if washed properly. To test for crease resistance, crumple a sample of fabric in your hand. If it springs back flat, it has a crease-resistant finish. If it retains the creases, it is not crease-resistant.]

mothproof
[This treatment is given only to fabrics which are normally attacked by moths.]

Fabrics can have a napped or brushed surface (for example, flannelette, winceyette), which gives extra warmth and softness. Napped fabrics are suitable for bed linen and nightwear.

Think and Do

1. Design a stripe, plaid, or check gingham fabric which you think would be suitable for a summer school uniform. Make a sketch of the style you would choose.

2. Copy the following diagram into your notebook and fill in the appropriate washing instructions for washing cotton and rayon articles with special finishes. The chart of wash care figures (page 48) will help you.

	MACHINE	HANDWASH
?	?	?
	?	

3. List four special finishes which can be applied to fabrics during manufacture. Which finishes would you require when choosing material for:
a. babies' clothes;
b. nightwear;
c. an anorak?
4. Explain what is meant by the following terms:
a. bulk yarn;
b. mercerized cotton;
c. P.V.C. fabric;
d. napped surface.
5. Copy the following sentences into your notebook. Say whether each one is *true* or *false.*
a. Woollen garments can be machine-washed.
b. Taffeta is a curly looking fabric that is woven with a looped yarn.
c. Winceyette is a warm fabric with a napped surface.
d. A garment labelled "drip-dry" does not require ironing.
e. Flannel is a hard fabric that resembles linen.
f. Nylon material can be permanently pleated.
6. Make a scrapbook of fabric samples. Underneath each sample describe:
a. the weave or knit;
b. the appearance of the fabric;
c. the fibre or mixture of fibres used in its manufacture.

7. Rearrange the following letters to give fabrics that have a "woollen" appearance.
a. LREVUO
b. GEESR
c. AIBEGNARD
d. LANEFNL
e. IWLTL
f. HRETBAAA
8. Find out the current price of:
a. a lightweight girdle in an elastomeric fibre;
b. a water-repellent raincoat;
c. a reel of mercerized cotton thread;
d. a denim waistcoat;
e. a pair of men's trousers with a heat-set permanent crease;
f. a metre of flame-resistant fabric suitable for a child's nightdress.
9. Copy the following chart into your notebook. Learn the various trademarks for special fabric finishes, so that you will be able to recognize them in the shops.

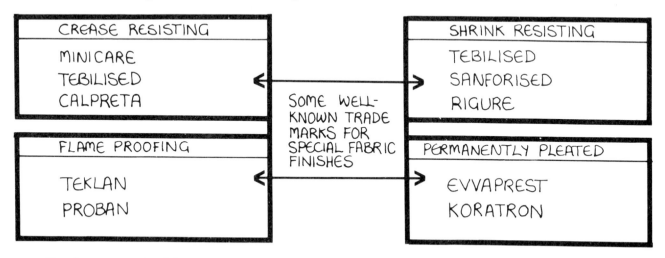

CREASE RESISTING

MINICARE
TEBILISED
CALPRETA

SHRINK RESISTING

TEBILISED
SANFORISED
RIGURE

SOME WELL-KNOWN TRADE MARKS FOR SPECIAL FABRIC FINISHES

FLAME PROOFING

TEKLAN
PROBAN

PERMANENTLY PLEATED

EVVAPREST
KORATRON

10. Say how you would:
a. test a fabric for crease-resistant properties;
b. recognize twill fabrics;
c. launder acetate fabrics with colours which are not fast at 40°C.

Part Three

About Sewing

Sewing equipment and using a sewing machine

There is a wide selection of sewing aids and accessories available for the home dressmaker and it is sometimes difficult to know which to choose. When starting to collect sewing equipment buy the best that you can afford. Tools of a good quality will last for many years if looked after properly, and they will help you to achieve that "professional" look with your sewing.

To begin home dressmaking you will need:

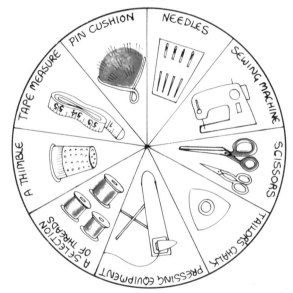

Needles Needles are numbered according to their thickness. A high number means a fine needle, and a low number means a coarse needle. An assortment of needles ranging from size 7 (for tacking) to size 10 (for fine sewing) is suitable. Needles can be:
long (these are called straw needles),
medium (these are called sharps),
short (these are called betweens).
It is possible to buy self-threading needles which have a partially opened "eye".

a self threading needle

In your needle case you will also need a bodkin for threading ribbon, tapes, or elastic, and a large-eyed darning needle. Crewel needles, which are medium length but with large eyes, are used for embroidery, and special needles can be bought for tapestry work.

Pins   Always choose rustless pins which have a sharp point. Pins vary in length from 12 mm to 44 mm but for ordinary sewing purposes use 25 mm or 30 mm. Glass-headed pins are expensive to buy but they are clearly seen and can be handled easily. It is sensible to store pins in a pin cushion. Pins which are kept in a tin or box become dirty quickly and are not as easy to pick up when required.

Scissors   You will need at least two pairs of scissors, which should be kept solely for sewing. A pair of good-quality cutting-scissors is essential. They should have long, sharp blades and should cut smoothly and evenly. A smaller pair with sharp points will also be needed for removing tacking stitches and close trimming work. Pinking shears that cut with a serrated edge to neaten the edges especially of fraying material, are useful but not essential. Do choose scissors that are comfortable to hold. It is possible to buy scissors that have moulded plastic handles and these are often kinder on the hands. Scissors can be bought for the left-handed as well as the right-handed person.

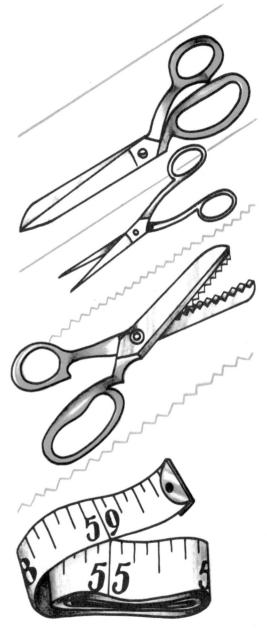

Tape measure   This can be made from cotton or fibre-glass but it is important to buy a good-quality tape that will not stretch. Choose one that has a metal tip at each end. This type will last longer. A flexible tape measure that is clearly marked on both sides is ideal.

Thimble   A thimble should feel comfortable and fit easily on the middle finger of the sewing hand. It can be steel-lined or nickel-plated.

Threads   It is most important in dressmaking to sew with a thread that has the same characteristics as the fabric. The thread should have the same stretch quality as the fabric, and it should be capable of being washed and ironed in a similar way. Remember that:

A natural material requires a natural thread (e.g. silk, cotton)

A synthetic material requires a synthetic thread (e.g. terylene, nylon)

It is possible to buy a multi-purpose sewing thread that can be safely used on natural and synthetic fabrics but this is more expensive to buy than ordinary thread.

Mercerized cotton is cotton that has been treated to give the thread extra strength and lustre.

The thickness of thread is denoted by the number gauge. A high number means a fine thread and a low number means a coarse thread. For ordinary sewing purposes, No. 40 thread will be suitable, but very fine materials may require Nos. 50 or 60. It is useful to remember that thread appears lighter when used, so always sew with a thread that is slightly darker than the fabric.

Ironing and pressing equipment   Nearly all irons are electric and have thermostatic heat controls. Some irons are light to handle but these may give a less satisfactory finish to a garment than a heavy iron. Try to choose a medium-weight iron that is comfortable to hold. An iron with a smaller base plate and a sharply pointed tip is good for ironing fine garments and getting into corners and gathers. A steam iron is useful because it can be used either dry or as a dampening agent when filled with water.

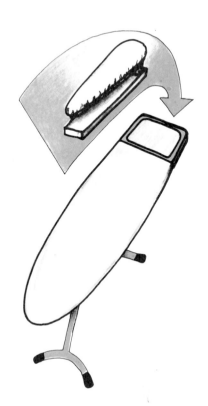

An ironing board should stand firmly, be easily assembled, and have adjustable height positions. A well-padded cover, which is removable for washing, is essential. A sleeve board can be bought separately or is sometimes part of an ironing board.

You will also need a piece of finely woven white sheeting for a pressing cloth. This should be smooth, unmarked, and have had all the dressing washed out so that it cannot mark the iron or fabric.

Tailor's chalk   This is used for marking material. It can be bought as squares, triangles, as powder or in pencil form, and is available in white and a variety of colours.

Sewing machine   You may be lucky enough to borrow a sewing machine but sooner or later you will want to have one of your own. A sewing machine is an expensive piece of equipment to buy, so it must be chosen with care. If you would like a sewing machine of your own but cannot afford a new electric model, why not consider buying a re-conditioned secondhand one?

There are many different makes and models of sewing machine available but they can all be divided into four groups.

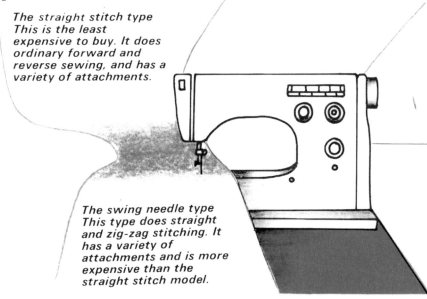

The straight stitch type
This is the least
expensive to buy. It does
ordinary forward and
reverse sewing, and has a
variety of attachments.

The swing needle type
This type does straight
and zig-zag stitching. It
has a variety of
attachments and is more
expensive than the
straight stitch model.

The swing needle
automatic
This type is more
expensive than the
ordinary swing needle
model. It does straight
and zig-zag stitching and
machine embroidery. A
variety of patterns can
be dialled, or selected by
means of a disc or cam.

The electronic type
This type is the most
expensive you can buy. It
has a transistorized
memory bank which is
programmed to produce
over 500 different
stitches in a variety of
patterns. It has a simple
push-button stitch-
selection panel.

Here are some points to help you when choosing a sewing machine.
1 Decide which type of machine will suit your needs best. If you intend using your machine only for sewing straight seams, then it is not necessary to buy a swing needle automatic or electronic version. A straight stitch or ordinary swing needle model will suffice. If, on the other hand, you are an accomplished dressmaker and require your sewing

machine to be versatile and to produce a variety of decorative and useful finishes, then consider buying a swing needle automatic or electronic model.

2 Sewing machines are available as portable or cabinet models. A portable, hand machine can be used on any suitable flat surface. A portable, electrically powered model can be used wherever there is a power point, but a cabinet model is too heavy to be moved around and must be kept in one particular place. If you are lucky enough to have a separate sewing room, or have space in a bedroom or utility room to make a sewing alcove, then you may wish to consider choosing a cabinet model. A sewing machine that is housed in a cabinet is disguised when not in use as an attractive piece of furniture, but these models are expensive to buy. If space is restricted, a portable machine that can be removed for storage is more convenient. Portable sewing machines are supplied with carrying cases that protect the machine when not in use.

3 When choosing a sewing machine, check that the controls are easy to adjust, and that the machine is not too noisy when operating.

4 Look for a good-quality model that can be serviced easily. Remember to ask if spare parts can be readily obtained.

5 It is a good idea to visit the sewing department of a large store and view the many different models available. Arrangements can usually be made to test a machine, either in the shop or at your home. Do check that the machine you are interested in has passed safety tests and that it is approved by consumer protection bodies. Why not read the appropriate article in the *Which?* magazine, before making a final choice?

A sewing machine should be cleaned and oiled regularly. The instruction booklet will tell you when and how to do this. A thorough service will also be necessary from time to time, if your machine is to be kept in good working order.

Before starting to sew you will have to choose a suitable thread and needle for your machine. The table overleaf may be used as a guide.

Kind of Material	Size of Needle		No. of Thread		No. of Stitches to 1 cm
	British	*Continental*	*British*	*Continental*	
Heavy fabrics, e.g. thick woollens, corduroy, velvet	16	100	40	67	5 or 6
Medium fabrics, e.g. cotton, linen, polyester, satin	14	90	50	84	4 or 5
Fine fabrics, e.g. lawn, crêpe, silk, lace	11	80	60	100	3 or 4

When you have fitted the correct needle, then you are ready to fill the bobbin and thread the machine. Your instruction booklet will tell you exactly how to do this. After threading, check that both threads (one from the bobbin and one from the reel) pass under the presser foot.

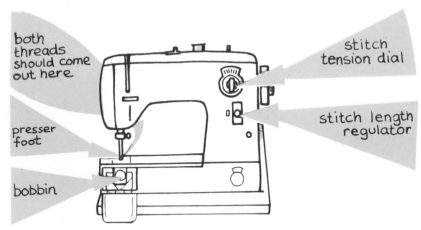

both threads should come out here

presser foot

bobbin

stitch tension dial

stitch length regulator

Always test the stitch size and tension before beginning to sew. This should be done on a scrap of double fabric. A stitch is formed by interlocking the two threads. A correctly formed stitch will look the same on both sides of the material.

This stitch is correctly formed.
Here the top tension is too tight.
Here the top tension is too loose.

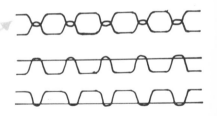

Before adjusting the tension, always check that the machine and bobbin have been threaded correctly. To alter the tension of the top thread, move the dial on the tension spring. The higher the number, the tighter the upper thread tension will be. If you cannot form a correct stitch by adjusting this dial, then check with your instruction booklet before trying to alter the tension on the bobbin. The stitch regulator will adjust the length of the stitch. If the fabric puckers during sewing, it could mean that the stitches are too small, so alter the stitch regulator.

Here are some stitch problems you may have, and hints on how to deal with them.

Uneven stitching
Check that
1.   the size of needle and thread is correct;
2.   the presser foot is down;
3.   the threading is correct;
4.   the bobbin is evenly filled;
5.   the fabric is not being pulled or pushed through the machine.

Bobbin thread breaking
Check that
1.   the lower tension is loose enough;
2.   the bobbin is correctly wound;
3.   the bobbin is not too full.

Skipped stitches
Check that
1.   the needle is firmly in position;
2.   the needle is sharp;
3.   the needle is the correct size.

Needle thread breaking
Check that
1.   the needle is correctly in position;
2.   the threading and tension are correct;
3.   the needle is the correct size;
4.   the needle is in good condition;
5.   the cotton is not caught behind the tension dial.

If these happen to you, *keep calm* and *be patient.* Read your instruction booklet carefully and carry on testing your stitching on a scrap of material until you are satisfied.

Before starting to machine, always:

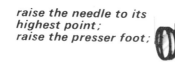

raise the needle to its highest point;
raise the presser foot;

insert the material from the front;
lower the presser foot;
lower the needle;
begin stitching.

When machining round a corner, always:

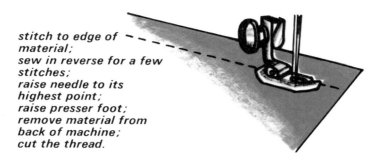

sew up to the corner;
leave the needle in the
material;
raise the presser foot;
swing the material
round;
lower the presser foot;
continue stitching.

When finishing machining, always:

stitch to edge of
material;
sew in reverse for a few
stitches;
raise needle to its
highest point;
raise presser foot;
remove material from
back of machine;
cut the thread.

Think and Do

1. Make a list of the equipment you would require for home dressmaking.

2. Prepare a class display on sewing machine attachments. Ask your teacher if she will arrange a demonstration on how each of the attachments works.

3. How would you correct each of the following faults on a sewing machine:

a. a looped stitch which forms on the underside of the fabric;

b. uneven stitching;

c. puckered material?

4. Make a list of articles which could be gaily decorated using machine embroidery.

5. In your own words, describe how you would:
a. machine round a corner;
b. alter the top thread tension on a sewing machine;
c. clean and oil a sewing machine.
6. Find out the current price of:
a. a pair of pinking shears;
b. a good-quality ironing board;
c. a bobbin of mercerized cotton;
d. a fibreglass tape measure with metal tips;
e. a packet of size 14 machine needles;
f. a swing needle sewing machine;
g. a bobbin of multi-purpose sewing thread;
h. a packet of self-threading needles.
7. Make a simple pin cushion using two circles of felt (10 cm diameter). Join the felt pieces with a hand-worked buttonhole stitch, and stuff with kapok, foam rubber, or old nylon stockings.
8. Copy out this crossword and complete it.

Clues across

1. A type of needle which is used for embroidery.
2. This will protect the sewing finger.
3. A suitable place to keep pins.

Clues down

1. This is used for marking material.
4. The name of a medium-sized needle.
5. This is used for threading ribbon and elastic.

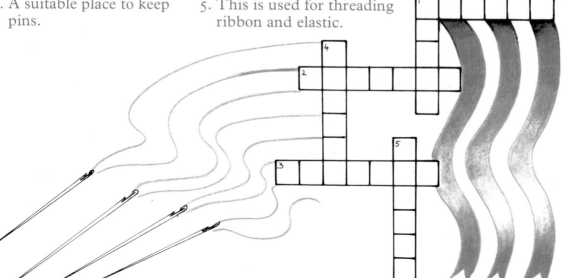

9. Copy the following diagram into your notebook. Write
a suitable sentence in each of the boxes.

TYPES OF SEWING MACHINE

STRAIGHT STITCH MODEL	ELECTRONIC MODEL
SWING NEEDLE MODEL	SWING NEEDLE AUTOMATIC

10. Sketch a trouser and tunic outfit which you would like
to make for yourself. Make a list of all the materials and
equipment you would require to make the outfit.

Understanding paper patterns

Commercial patterns are a marvellous aid for the home dressmaker. Today's range of patterns is reliable and easy to use. Whether you require a simple, casual style or an elaborate, fashionable creation, there is a wide choice available, and all patterns are produced in a range of sizes for different types of figures.

If you are a beginner at dressmaking, start by choosing a simple design. Many patterns are labelled "easy-to-make", and these are always safe to choose. Remember to consider your figure when choosing a style, and try to pick a pattern that will enhance your good features and disguise any bad ones (See Chapter 3).

Pattern size measurements are printed on the back of the pattern envelope and these are standardized for all pattern firms. Decide first which figure type you require. This is usually determined by the height and back waist length measurement. Then choose the correct size in the appropriate figure type.

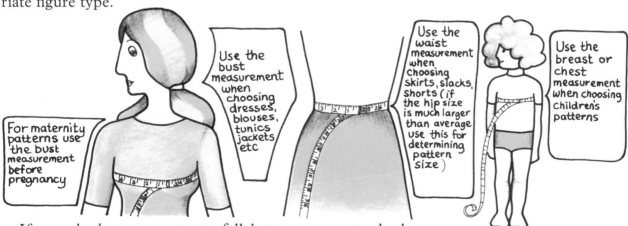

For maternity patterns use the bust measurement before pregnancy

Use the bust measurement when choosing dresses, blouses, tunics, jackets etc

Use the waist measurement when choosing skirts, slacks, shorts (if the hip size is much larger than average use this for determining pattern size)

Use the breast or chest measurement when choosing children's patterns

If your body measurements fall between two standard measurements, choose the larger of the two. It is easier to reduce a pattern than to enlarge it. Most paper patterns indicate where pieces should be shortened or lengthened.

This is shown by two continuous lines. Any alterations to the pattern pieces should be made along these lines, so that the balance of the garment is not destroyed.

Here are some points to help you when altering the size of a paper pattern.

1 To reduce any particular measurement, make a pleat by creasing the pattern neatly in the required position. The depth of the pleat should be half the amount to be reduced. Alterations in the width of a pattern should be divided equally between front/back and left/right sides of the garment. Sleeve width is altered down the centre.

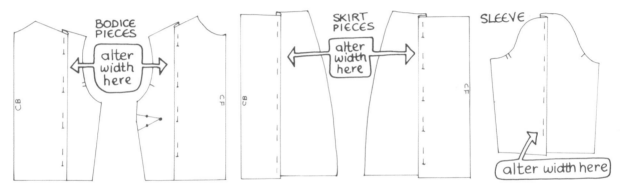

2 To shorten a bodice piece, make the correct pleat below the bust line. Skirt pieces are shortened between the hip and hem measurement. Alterations in the length of a sleeve are divided equally between shoulder/elbow and elbow/ wrist positions.

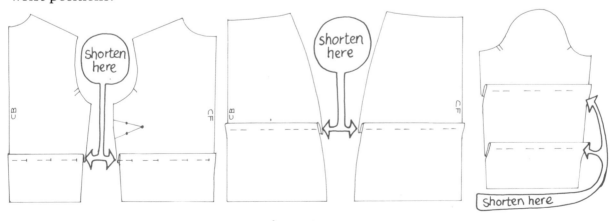

3 To enlarge any particular measurement, cut through the pattern and insert an extra strip of paper to give the required width. Remember to divide the extra width equally between front/back and left/right sides of the garment. Sleeve width is increased from the shoulder to the wrist.

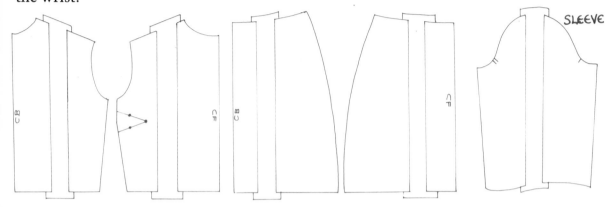

4 To lengthen a bodice piece, make the insertion below the bust line. Skirts are lengthened between the hip and hem measurement. Alterations in the length of a sleeve are divided equally between shoulder/elbow and elbow/wrist positions.

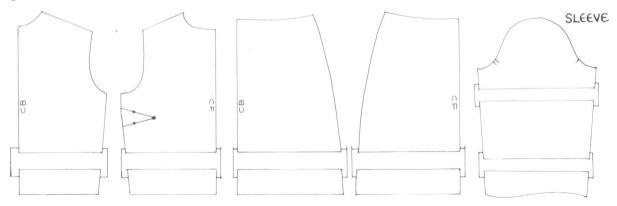

5 If a sleeve is taken in or widened, the armhole must be adjusted accordingly.
6 If the waist edge of a bodice is reduced or enlarged, the waist edge of the skirt must be adjusted also.
7 A waist measurement can be reduced by taking in the

side seams, or by enlarging or introducing darts. It can be enlarged by letting out darts or by adding to the side seams.

Having selected the pattern you require, then you can choose a fabric. Fabrics are sold in the following widths. Check the grid on the back of the pattern to find out how much fabric you will need to buy. The grid will list the various styles included in the pattern (these are usually referred to as VIEW 1, VIEW 2, VIEW 3, etc.) and will then give a choice of fabric widths. Select the view and fabric width required. Read along the line until you come to the size of garment you are making. The amount of fabric required will be indicated. If the fabric chosen has a napped or brushed surface, remember to look for a "with nap" measurement.

When choosing a fabric, do:

90 cm
115 cm
120 cm
140 cm
150 cm

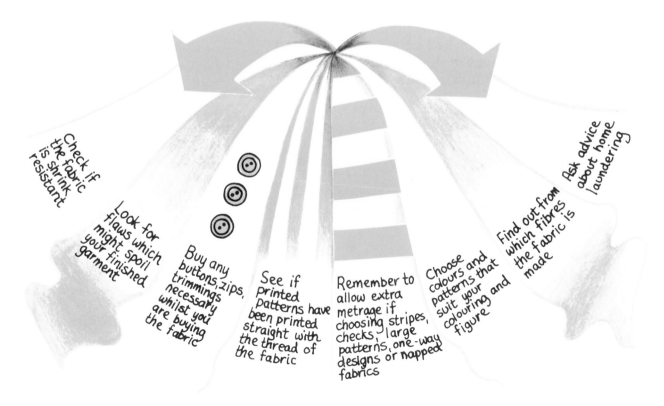

Check if the fabric is shrink resistant

Look for flaws which might spoil your finished garment

Buy any buttons, zips, trimmings necessary whilst you are buying the fabric

See if printed patterns have been printed straight with the thread of the fabric

Remember to allow extra metrage if choosing stripes, checks, large patterns, one-way designs or napped fabrics

Choose colours and patterns that suit your colouring and figure

Find out from which fibres the fabric is made

Ask advice about home laundering

Preparations for cutting out

1 Unpack the paper pattern and sort out which pattern pieces you will require.

2 If you need to alter any particular measurement, make the necessary adjustments to the paper pattern now.

3 Look at the suggested pattern layouts and choose the correct one for your style, fabric width, and size.

4 Press the fabric carefully. Loosely woven woollen fabric should be shrunk slightly by pressing with a damp cloth. Allow the fabric to dry before cutting out.

5 Straighten the ends of the fabric. Either draw a thread and cut along the thread line, or cut the ends straight with the pattern. It is also helpful to pull the fabric on the bias. This will straighten the grain.

6 Fold the fabric, as directed by the pattern layout, and spread it smoothly on the cutting-out table. Fabric can be folded so that the fold lies:

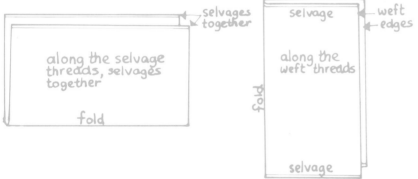

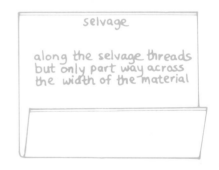

Sometimes pattern pieces are cut from single thickness of material, and the fabric is opened out, right side upwards.

7 Study the key to the symbols and pattern markings. These marks are important and are meant to guide you when cutting and sewing the garment. The chart overleaf shows you the main symbols and pattern markings found on commercial patterns. Some patterns are marked with tiny holes or perforations, instead of lines. The meaning for each perforated symbol is the same as for the printed form, but if in doubt refer to the key.

8 Lay the pattern pieces on the fabric, as directed by the layout. Pin securely in position. Place the pins diagonally

Pattern marking or symbol	Meaning
═══════════	Lengthen or shorten the pattern here.
←──────────→	The straight of the grain
↓──────────↓	Lay on the folded edge of the fabric.
✄	Cutting line
▷▼▼▼▼▼▼▼▷	Position and size of zip opening
✂ – – – – – –	Fitting or seam line
◆ ⬥ ────────	These show where one piece should join on to another. They are called BALANCE MARKS.
••••	Dart
•──────────•	Centre or fold line
⬠	Pleat
⬤ (button)	Position and size of button
⊢──────⊣	Position and size of buttonhole
──────────→	Stitch in direction of arrow.

or at right angles to the pattern edge, every 10 to 15 cm. Pin securely through the paper pattern and through both pieces of fabric. Check that the pins are *inside* the cutting line of the pattern.

You are now ready for cutting out. Make one last check of the layout.

a Are the necessary pieces to the fold?

b Is the straight thread of the material parallel with marking?

c Is there enough space for pieces which have to be cut a second time?

d Have the correct pieces been placed on double/ single thickness of material?

How to cut out

Always use a good pair of cutting shears. Spread the left hand flat to keep the pattern and fabric in position, and cut with long, even strokes round each of the pattern pieces. Most commercial patterns show the cutting line as a thick black line, but with perforated patterns the cutting line is around the edge of each pattern piece. Do not be tempted to lift up the fabric during cutting. All balance marks should be cut *outwards*, so that the seam allowance is not spoiled. This may be needed if the garment has to be let out during fitting.

Leave the pattern pieces pinned to the fabric unless you need to cut a second, reversed piece on single-thickness fabric.

How to mark out

Before the pattern is removed from the fabric, you will need to transfer these from the pattern to the fabric.

All fitting lines
The centre lines
} can be transferred by using special dressmaker's carbon paper, a tracing wheel, or tailor's chalk. The lines are then marked with straight tacking stitches.

All balance marks
The position of darts, pleats, and tucks
The position of openings and pockets
The position of buttons and buttonholes
are marked with tailor's tacks [see page 110].

When all pattern lines and markings have been transferred to the fabric, the pattern pieces can be carefully removed, smoothed flat, and replaced in the pattern envelope. You are now ready to assemble the garment.

How to fit a garment

In order to obtain a well-fitting garment, it is necessary to tack up the various pieces and try the garment on before machining. Any adjustments can then be dealt with before the garment is finally sewn. When tacking:

a pin and tack darts and seams after matching fitting lines and balance marks;

b attach skirt pieces to the bodice;

c tack up the sleeves but do not join to the bodice.

When trying on for fitting, put the garment on inside out. It is then much easier to adjust seams and darts. Try to get a friend to help you and check that:

a the garment hangs correctly;

b the waistline is in the correct position;

c the darts are the right size and fit well;

d the shoulder seams lie well;

e the neckline lies flat and is not loose;

f the garment is neither too loose nor too tight;

g the sleeves hang correctly and do not wrinkle or pucker around the armhole.

Any necessary adjustments should be marked with pins, and the garment carefully removed. Re-tack the garment using the fitting pins as a guide. Check the fit of the garment once more, and if you are satisfied, then prepare to machine.

Order of work for making up a garment

A garment is constructed or built up in the following way:

12 Sew on buttons, press studs, hooks and eyes.

11 Press.

10 Turn up the hem.

9 Insert zips or side plackets.

8 Attach skirt to bodice.

7 Sew sleeves, make cuffs. Insert into bodice.

6 Sew side seams.

5 Complete front/back neck facing, and bound button-holes.

4 Prepare and attach collar.

3 Attach pockets, work buttonholes, make belts.

2 Join shoulder seams.

1 Sew darts, pleats, or tucks.

Raglan sleeves are inserted here

If using a front/back zip insert here

start here

Think and Do

1. The diagram shows a front bodice pattern piece. In your notebook, explain the meaning of each of the pattern markings and say how you would transfer them to the fabric.

2. In your notebook, list some points to remember when buying and using commercial patterns.

3. Which body measurement is most important when buying a pattern for:

a. a dress;

b. a skirt;

c. a maternity smock;

d. a child's playsuit;

e. a pair of slacks;

f. a blouse?

4. Say how you would:

a. reduce a waist measurement;

b. shrink a loosely woven woollen fabric;

c. transfer fitting lines from a paper pattern.

5. Copy the diagram of a back bodice pattern into your notebook. Explain how you would:

a. lengthen it;

b. reduce its width.

6. Copy out the following sentences into your notebook. Say whether each one is *true* or *false*.

a. Balance marks show where one pattern piece should join another.

b. The cutting line on a paper pattern is shown by a dotted, thin line.

c. Side seams should be sewn before a collar is attached.

d. Fabric can be straightened by drawing a thread.

e. Notches should always be cut inwards.

f. If your body measurements fall between two standard measurements, you should always choose the larger of the two when buying a paper pattern.

7. Copy the diagram of pattern symbols and markings (page 104) into your notebook.

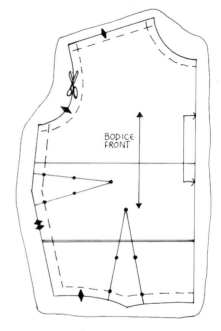

BODICE FRONT

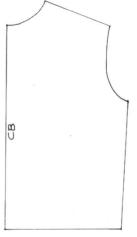

CB

8. Using the details given below, calculate the following.

a. The amount of 90 cm wide fabric that is needed to make dress A for a child whose chest size is 73 cm.

b. The amount of 150 cm wide fabric that is needed to make dress B in size 66 cm.

Chest (cm)	66	69	73	76	81
Size code	7	8	10	12	14

Dress A

	66	69	73	76	81
90 cm	1,85	2,15	2,30	2,50	2,60 metres
115 cm	1,70	1,70	1,70	1,80	1,95 metres
150 cm	1,25	1,25	1,35	1,50	1,60 metres

Dress B

	66	69	73	76	81
90 cm	1,85	1,95	1,95	2,05	2,15 metres
115 cm	1,25	1,35	1,70	1,80	1,80 metres
150 cm	1,15	1,15	1,15	1,25	1,25 metres

9. Give advice on fitting a garment.

10. Copy out the following crossword and complete it.

Clues across

1. When a sleeve piece is reduced or enlarged, this must be adjusted.
2. ⌐——↓ means place to a ....
3. A ...... is when a garment is tacked up and tried on, before machining.

Clues down

4. Seam lines can be transferred to fabric using this.
5. •——•
6. This measurement is used when choosing children's clothes.

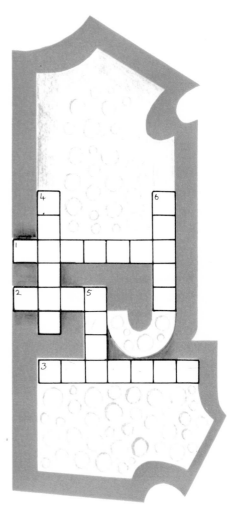

Hand stitching and sewing seams

Hand stitching has many uses. It can:

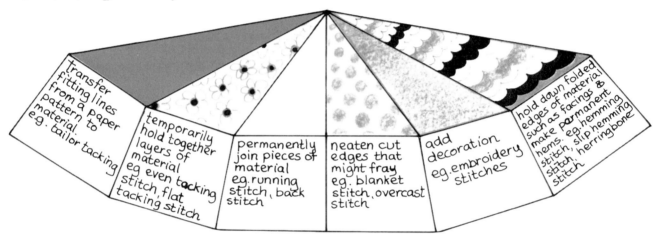

transfer fitting lines from a paper pattern to material. e.g. tailor tacking

temporarily hold together layers of material eg even tacking stitch, flat tacking stitch

permanently join pieces of material eg.running stitch, back stitch

neaten cut edges that might fray eg. blanket stitch, overcast stitch

add decoration eg.embroidery stitches

hold down folded edges of material such as facings & hems: make permanent hems. eg.hemming stitch, slip hemming stitch, herringbone stitch

Tailor tacking   These stitches are used to transfer marks from a paper pattern to the material. Sew with a double length of tacking thread. Make a small stitch through the centre of the hole on the paper pattern and through both layers of material. Stitch again into the same hole but do not pull the thread through tightly. Leave a loop. When all the balance marks from the paper pattern have been tailor tacked, remove the pins, snip between the loops, and carefully lift the pattern up. Separate the two layers of material and cut through the stitches, leaving half of the tacking thread in each piece of material.

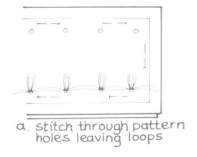

a. stitch through pattern holes leaving loops

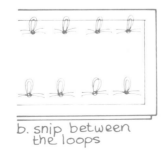

b. snip between the loops

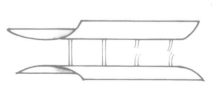

c. separate the two layers of material and cut through stitches

It is possible to buy a sewing machine that will work machined tailor's tacks.

Even tacking stitch   Begin with a knot and sew with a single thickness of tacking thread. Work even tacking stitches, about 1 cm long, and finish by sewing over the last stitch twice. When tacking seams which will take a lot of strain during fitting, insert a few back stitches to give firmness and added strength.

even tacking stitch

Flat tacking stitch   This stitch is stronger than an even tacking stitch. Begin with a knot and sew with a single thickness of tacking thread. Make long and short stitches alternately. Finish by sewing over the last stitch twice.

flat tacking stitch

Running stitch   This stitch is used for sewing seams and for gathering. Start with two stitches worked on top of each other. This will hold the thread firmly in position. Then weave the needle in and out of the material, making small, even stitches. Finish by sewing over the last stitch twice.

running stitch

Back stitch   This is a firm stitch which resembles machine stitching. Start with two stitches worked on top of each other. Make a running stitch. Take the needle backwards and sew just in front of the preceding stitch, bringing the needle out the length of the stitch beyond the thread. Finish by sewing over the last stitch twice.

back stitch

Hemming stitch   This stitch is used for holding down folded edges, for example, facings, and for making hems. Join the thread by running the needle through the fold, from left to right. Make small, slanting stitches, sewing into the single material and through the fold. The stitches should be even in size and fairly loose. A tight hemming stitch will pull the material and leave a mark on the right side. Finish by sewing over the last stitch twice.

hemming stitch

Slip-hemming stitch   This is an invisible way of sewing a hem. Work with the hem folded away from you. Join the thread by running the needle through the fold, from left to right. Pick up a single thread from the material, then slip the needle $\frac{1}{2}$ cm along the fold. Pick up another thread and continue stitching along the fold. Do not pull the thread tightly. Finish by sewing two back stitches in the fold or hem.

slip-hemming stitch

Herringbone stitch   This stitch is used for holding down single hems on materials that do not fray, and it is worked from left to right. Join the thread by sewing a back stitch in the hem. Pick up one or two threads from the material, inserting the needle from right to left. Then sew a small stitch in the hem, again pulling the needle from right to left. Continue across the hem. Each stitch will form a cross and lie at right angles to the previous stitch. Finish with a back stitch in the hem. Herringbone stitch can also be used as an embroidery stitch.

herringbone stitch

Blanket stitch This stitch is used for neatening raw edges on seams, and is worked from left to right. Join the thread by sewing a back stitch. Put the needle in the material at right angles to the raw edge. The thread will form a loop **under** the needle. Pull the needle through. Continue sewing along the raw edge. Finish with a back stitch. Blanket stitch can also be used as an embroidery stitch.

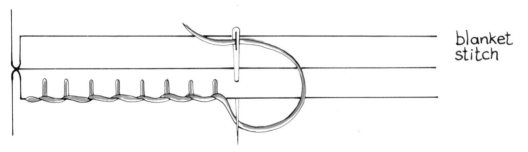

blanket stitch

Overcast stitch This stitch is used for neatening raw edges that might fray, and it is worked from left to right on either single or double material. Join the thread by sewing a back stitch, then work small, evenly spaced, slanting stitches along the cut edge. Finish with a back stitch.

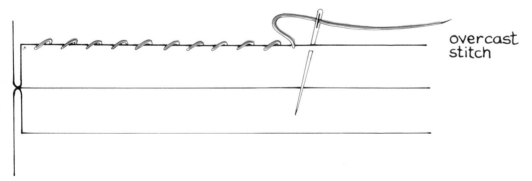

overcast stitch

Embroidery stitches Embroidery stitches can be worked by hand, or by using a swing needle automatic or electronic sewing machine. Embroidery can be purely a decorative feature, or it can have a practical use, for example, the inserting of lace edges on garments.

Here are some simple hand embroidery stitches for you
to try.

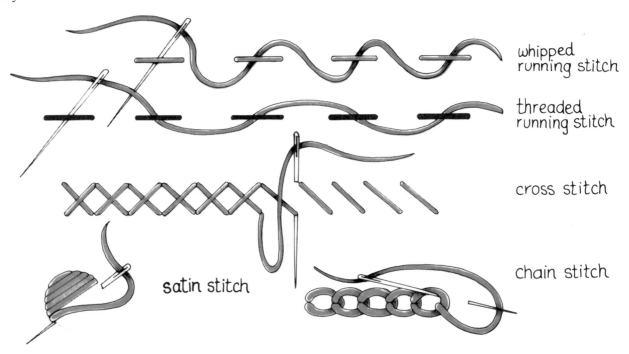

whipped
running stitch

threaded
running stitch

cross stitch

chain stitch

satin stitch

Here are some examples of machine embroidery.

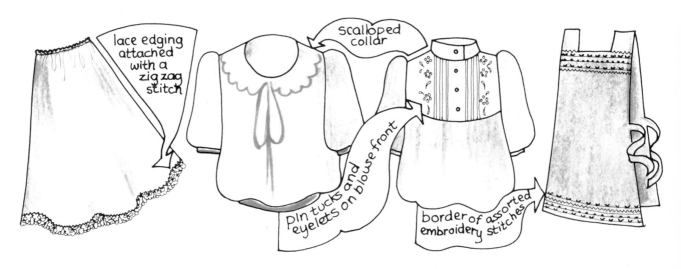

lace edging
attached
with a
zig zag
stitch

scalloped
collar

pin tucks and
eyelets on blouse front

border of assorted
embroidery stitches

Seams

Seams are used to join pieces of material together. The four main seams used in dressmaking are:

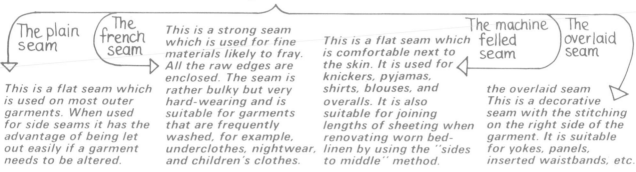

The plain seam

The french seam

This is a strong seam which is used for fine materials likely to fray. All the raw edges are enclosed. The seam is rather bulky but very hard-wearing and is suitable for garments that are frequently washed, for example, underclothes, nightwear, and children's clothes.

The machine felled seam

The overlaid seam

This is a flat seam which is used on most outer garments. When used for side seams it has the advantage of being let out easily if a garment needs to be altered.

This is a flat seam which is comfortable next to the skin. It is used for knickers, pyjamas, shirts, blouses, and overalls. It is also suitable for joining lengths of sheeting when renovating worn bed-linen by using the "sides to middle" method.

the overlaid seam This is a decorative seam with the stitching on the right side of the garment. It is suitable for yokes, panels, inserted waistbands, etc.

How to make a plain seam

1 Pin the two pieces of material together, matching balance marks and placing the right sides together.
2 Tack along the fitting line.
3 Remove the pins and machine from the top of the seam, just on the outside of the tacking line.
4 Remove the tacking and press the seam open, starting from the bottom.
5 Neaten the seam edges to prevent fraying by using one of the following methods.

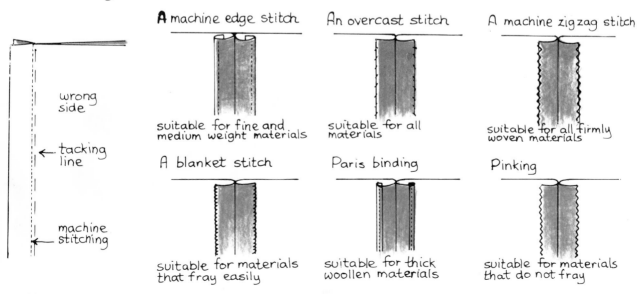

wrong side

tacking line

machine stitching

A machine edge stitch
suitable for fine and medium weight materials

An overcast stitch
suitable for all materials

A machine zigzag stitch
suitable for all firmly woven materials

A blanket stitch
suitable for materials that fray easily

Paris binding
suitable for thick woollen materials

Pinking
suitable for materials that do not fray

How to make a french seam

1 Pin the two pieces of material together, matching balance marks and placing the wrong sides together.

2 Tack along the fitting line. Remove the pins.

3 Machine from the top of the seam $\frac{1}{4}$ or $\frac{1}{2}$ cm outside the fitting line, according to the required width of the finished seam.

4 Remove the tacking and press the seam open, starting from the bottom.

5 Trim turnings to less than the finished width of seam.

6 Turn garment so that the right sides are together. Pin, tack, and machine on the fitting line, enclosing all the raw edges.

7 Press the finished seam towards the back of the garment.

How to make a machine-felled or double-machined seam

1 Pin the two pieces of material together, matching balance marks and placing the right sides together.

2 Tack along the fitting line. Remove the pins.

3 Machine from the top of the seam just on the outside of the tacking line.

4 Trim one seam allowance to $\frac{1}{2}$ cm and the other to 1 cm. Press the seam flat.

5 Fold the wider seam allowance over the narrower one, turning the edge under.

6 Pin, tack, and machine close to the edge.

This seam can be sewn on the outside or inside of a garment. To make a machine-felled seam which is topstitched on the outside of a garment, as in denim clothes, make the plain seam with the wrong sides inside.

How to make an overlaid seam

1 Using the overlaying piece of material, fold the seam allowance to the wrong side. Pin and tack so that the fitting line is directly on the edge.

2 Lay this piece on to the underlying material, matching balance marks and fitting lines, and with right sides outside.

3 Pin, tack, and machine close to the edge.

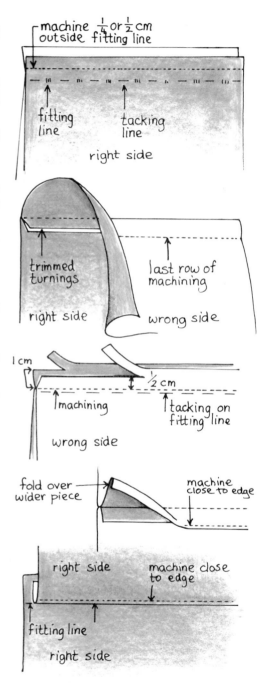

4 Trim the turnings and neaten the raw edges with zig-zag, overcast, or blanket stitches.

Here are some general points to help you when sewing seams.

1 Do not machine over tacking stitches. This will make the tacking difficult to remove, and strain may be put on the material. It is better to machine just on the outside of the tacking line. (If you machine on the inside of the tacking line, the garment will be too small.)

2 Always remove pins and tacking stitches before pressing a seam flat. If an impression of the seam edges is apparent on the right side of the garment, lay a damp cloth under the seam edges on the wrong side and press again.

3 Seam lines should be smooth. Where seams are shaped, for example, at waist or around necklines and sleeves, the seam line should be curved slowly and evenly. Sharp angles in a seam will leave puckers and unsightly points.

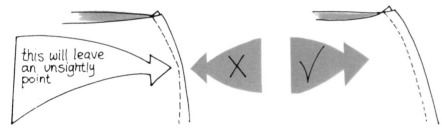

Curved seams should be snipped to the stitching line before being pressed flat.

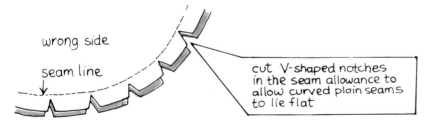

4 Bulky seams should be trimmed to be as neat and inconspicuous as possible.

5 The ends of seams should be fastened securely by machining in reverse or tying with a knot.

Think and Do

1. Imagine that you are going to make a decorated tray-cloth using checked gingham material. In your notebook work out a pattern using simple hand-embroidery stitches. Name the stitches you plan to use and suggest a suitable colour scheme.

2. Describe three ways of neatening the edges on a plain seam. Illustrate your answer where possible. Say where you would use each of the methods you have mentioned.

3. A machine zig-zag stitch can be used in several different ways. Make a list of its many uses in dressmaking.

4. Say how you would:
a. machine a curved seam;
b. remove the impression of seam edges showing on the right side of a garment;
c. fasten the thread securely after sewing a seam.

5. Copy the following diagram into your notebook and write a suitable sentence in each of the boxes.

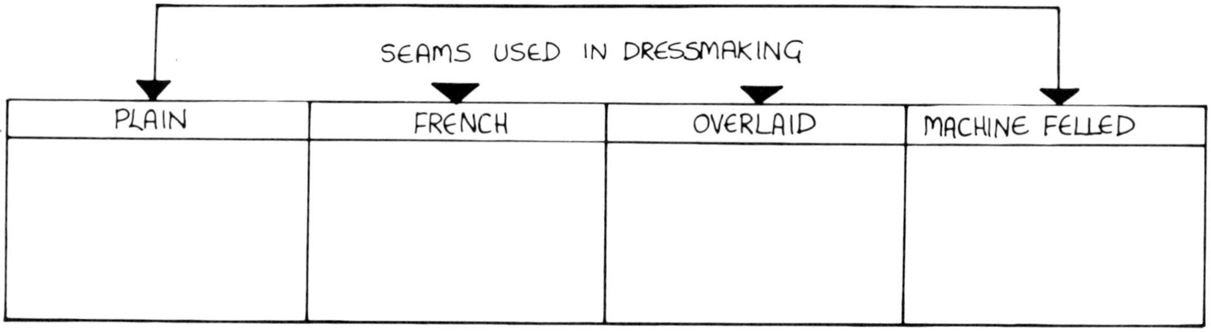

PLAIN	FRENCH	OVERLAID	MACHINE FELLED

SEAMS USED IN DRESSMAKING

6. Say what is meant by the following terms:
a. fitting line;
b. french seam;
c. tailor tack;
d. blanket stitch.

7. Suggest a suitable seam for each of the following:
a. the leg seams in a pair of pyjama trousers;

b. the side seams on a child's towelling playsuit;

c. setting a sleeve into a cotton blouse;

d. the side seams on a nylon underslip;

e. a shaped waist seam on a cotton dress;

f. the yoke seam on a shirt blouse.

8. Copy the following sentences into your notebook. Say whether each one is *true* or *false*.

a. A running stitch is used for gathering.

b. A straight stitch sewing machine can be used for machine embroidery.

c. Alternate long and short stitches are firmer than even tacking stitches.

d. Slip hemming is an invisible way of sewing a hem.

e. Blanket stitch is worked from right to left.

f. Tailor's tacks are used to transfer marks from a paper pattern to the material.

9. How would you make a machine-felled seam? Give some general points to remember when sewing seams.

10. Show two ways in which running stitches can be used to form a border design.

Disposal of fullness and edge finishes

Disposal of fullness
Fullness in a garment can be removed by using:

Darts
A dart is made by enclosing fullness in a wedge-shaped piece of material. This method is used on shoulders and underarm seams, and at the waist on bodices and skirts. The fitting line for a dart is transferred from the paper pattern to the material by means of tailor's tacks.

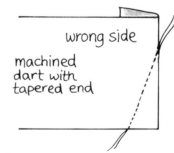

1 Pin and tack along the fitting line of the dart, with right sides facing. Remove the pins.

2 Machine just on the inside of the tacking line, starting at the widest part of the dart. Taper the end of the dart gently, making the last few stitches lie on the fold. Secure ends of dart by tying with a knot or sewing a double stitch by hand.

3 Remove the tacking.

4 Press dart flat in one of the following positions:

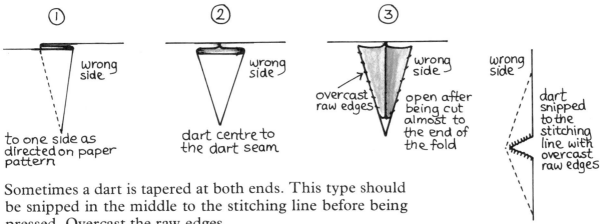

Sometimes a dart is tapered at both ends. This type should be snipped in the middle to the stitching line before being pressed. Overcast the raw edges.

A paper pattern will state clearly how each dart should be pressed, but here are a few general points to help you.

1 Narrow darts should be pressed to one side. Waist darts are usually pressed towards the centre front or centre back. Underarm darts are pressed towards the waistline and shoulder darts towards the neck edge.

2 For wide darts or for thick fabric, slash the dart down the centre fold and press open, as in Fig. 3.

3 A double-pointed dart is used for garments which do not have a waist seam.

Gathers

Gathers are used to distribute fullness in a decorative way. They are found on yokes, skirts which are set into waist seams, sleeve heads, and cuffs.

1 Make two rows of running stitches just above the fitting line. Each row should begin with a secure back stitch.

2 Pull both threads until the material is the length you require. Temporarily secure the threads by winding around a pin.

3 Arrange the gathers evenly. Pin the gathered material to the band, yoke or bodice, taking care to match balance marks. Tack along the fitting line. Remove the pins. (Gathered pieces can be inserted with a plain or overlaid seam.)

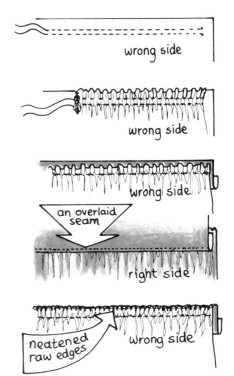

4 Machine just above the fitting line. Remove tacking and gathering threads. Raw edges should be neatened with zig-zag, overcast, or blanket stitches.

When setting a gathered piece of material into a band, join the two pieces with a plain seam. Trim the turnings and press the band away from the gathers. Fold the band over to the wrong side of the garment. Fold under a narrow hem and hem stitch along the sewing line.

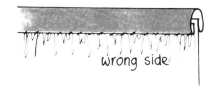

Here are some general points to help you when gathering.
1 If using a sewing machine for gathering, do use a long stitch and a loose top tension.
2 Always machine with the gathered piece uppermost. The gathers can then be eased evenly through the sewing machine.

Tucks

Tucks are another decorative way of removing fullness from a garment. They resemble pleats but are formed from double thickness of material and are usually stitched down their entire length. Tucks can vary in width from $1\frac{1}{2}$ mm to 2 cm. Tiny tucks are called pin tucks.

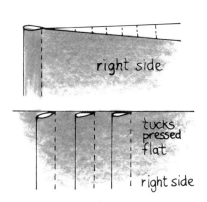

1 Always allow twice the width of tuck when you are calculating the amount of material needed; for example, for a group of 10 tucks, $\frac{1}{2}$ cm wide, allow $10\ (\frac{1}{2} \times 2) = 10$ cm material.
2 Fold the first tuck on the straight grain of the material, with the wrong sides facing. Pin, tack, and machine the tuck in position.
3 Remove the tacking.
4 Press tuck away from the centre of the garment.

Here are some general points to help you when making tucks.
1 A notched tuck marker, cut from a piece of cardboard, is useful for measuring the spacing and width of each tuck.
2 Pin tucks can be machined after each tuck has been measured with a marker and pressed in position. It is not necessary to tack them first.
3 Tucks should always be made along the straight grain of the material and they should lie parallel to each other.
4 Make each tuck in turn. Sew and press before making

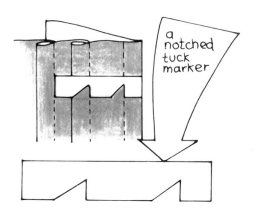

the next tuck. This will help to give a good finished appearance.

5 Always machine tucks from the bottom upwards.

6 All tucks should be pressed in the same direction.

Pleats

Pleats are folds made from treble thickness of material, which are usually stitched part way down the garment. They are found in skirts. The extra width at the bottom of the pleat allows for easier movement, and the stitched top of the pleat is enclosed into a seam at the waist. There are three main types of pleat.

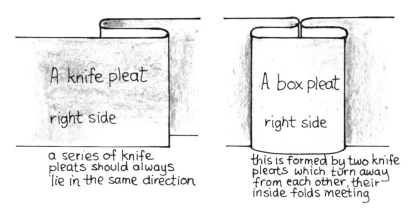

A knife pleat

right side

a series of knife pleats should always lie in the same direction

A box pleat

right side

this is formed by two knife pleats which turn away from each other, their inside folds meeting

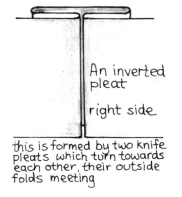

An inverted pleat

right side

this is formed by two knife pleats which turn towards each other, their outside folds meeting

1 Always allow three times the width of each pleat, when calculating the amount of material needed, for example, for a group of 4 knife pleats, 8 cm wide, allow 4 (8 × 3) = 96 cm material.

2 Balance marks showing the fold line of each pleat should be transferred from the paper pattern to the material. All pleats, except for flared knife pleats, should be on the straight grain of the material.

3 Matching balance marks, fold, pin and tack each pleat. It is a good idea to anchor one end of the pleat with a pin, while the rest of the pleat is being folded in position.

4 Press lightly using a damp cloth and a warm iron.

5 Machine the pleats in position, working from the bottom of each pleat upwards. The seam above each pleat may be plain or overlaid.

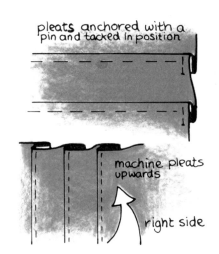

pleats anchored with a pin and tacked in position

machine pleats upwards

right side

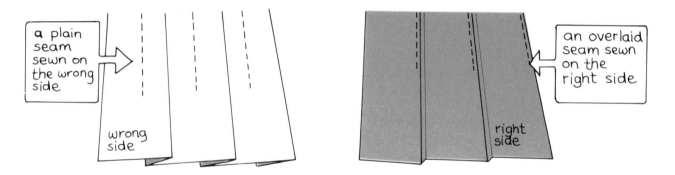

Here are some general points to help you when making pleats.

1 Always work on a flat surface when arranging pleats in position.

2 When pinning and tacking pleats, keep checking to see that the upper and lower edges of material are straight.

3 Pleats which are to fall loosely from the waist can be held securely in position with a row of machining just above the waist seam.

4 An inverted pleat can have a separate underlay.

5 Pleats in very thick material can be trimmed at the back. This avoids bulk along the hip and waist lines.

6 The tops of pleats can be strengthened by working bar or arrowhead tacks.

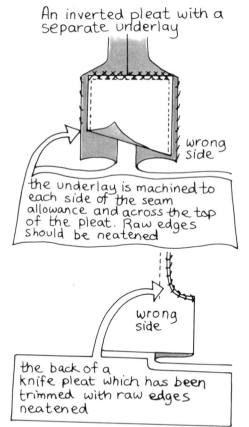

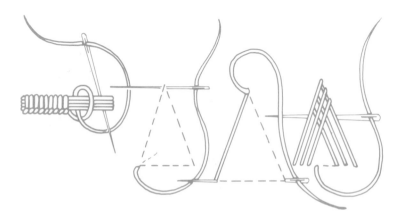

7 Do check that all pins, tailor's tacks, and tacking thread are removed before the pleats are finally pressed.

Edge finishes

Raw edges can be finished in many different ways depending on whether the edge is meant to be invisible or is intended to be a decorative addition to a garment.

Hems

The length of a garment will be dictated by the current trend in fashion but it is important that a hem lies flat and is even all the way round. A neat and immaculate hem line should be the aim of all dressmakers. Before turning a hem, the length should be checked. The garment should be tried on, and the position of the hem line marked with tailor's chalk or pins, by another person. A stick which is marked at regular intervals, is a useful aid when levelling hems. The position of the hem line or fitting line should then be marked with flat tacking stitches.

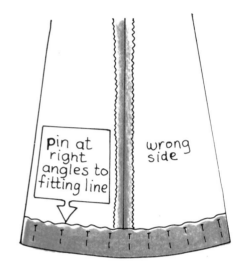

1 Lay the garment flat on the wrong side.
2 Fold over the hem allowance along the fitting line.
3 Pin at right angles to the fitting line.
4 With a loose stitch, tack 1 cm from the fitting line.
5 Allowing approximately 5 cm width for the hem, cut away any excess material. (On children's clothes a hem of up to 10 cm can be allowed.)
6 Press the hem lightly on the wrong side.
7 Neaten the raw edge using one of the methods shown overleaf.

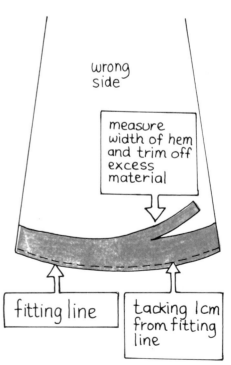

A paper pattern will state how a hem should be finished, but here are a few general points to help you.
1 A straight plain hem, as in method 1, is suitable for lightweight fabrics, where the skirt is not flared.
2 When a skirt is flared, use methods 2 or 6. If the fabric is thin, finish the hem as in method 6.
3 A bound hem is suitable for thick fabrics which fray easily.
4 A herring-boned hem is used for thick fabrics which do not fray.
5 Fullness can be "shrunk" away on woollen fabrics. The edge can then be finished by methods 3 or 4.
6 A false hem is used where there is an inadequate hem

① A STRAIGHT PLAIN HEM

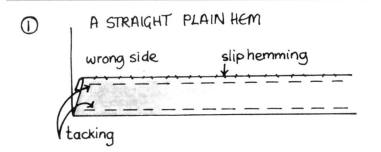

wrong side   slip hemming

tacking

Turn the raw edge under
and tack into position.
Slip-hem along the top
fold. Remove tacking
thread and press well on
the wrong side.

② A FLARED PLAIN HEM

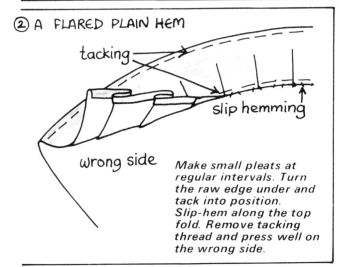

tacking

slip hemming

wrong side

wrong side

Make small pleats at
regular intervals. Turn
the raw edge under and
tack into position.
Slip-hem along the top
fold. Remove tacking
thread and press well on
the wrong side.

③ A "SHRUNK" HEM (suitable for woollen materials)

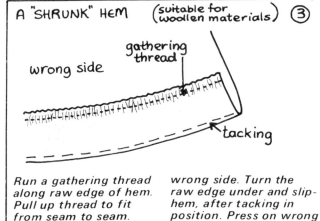

wrong side   gathering thread

tacking

Run a gathering thread
along raw edge of hem.
Pull up thread to fit
from seam to seam.
Using a damp cloth and
hot iron, press on the
wrong side. Turn the
raw edge under and slip-
hem, after tacking in
position. Press on wrong
side.

④ A HEM EDGED WITH PARIS BINDING

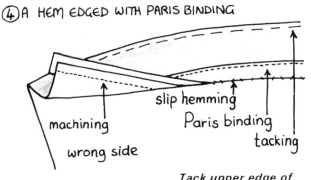

machining   slip hemming
                   Paris binding
wrong side   tacking

Tack binding on right
side of hem with binding
overlapping raw edge.
Machine binding through
single thickness of hem.

Tack upper edge of
binding to garment and
slip-hem in position.
Remove tacking thread
and press well on the
wrong side.

⑤ A HERRINGBONED HEM (suitable for thick fabrics)

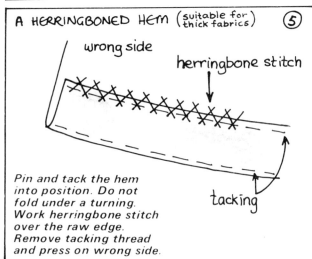

wrong side   herringbone stitch

tacking

Pin and tack the hem
into position. Do not
fold under a turning.
Work herringbone stitch
over the raw edge.
Remove tacking thread
and press on wrong side.

⑥ A NARROW HEM (suitable for very full skirts)

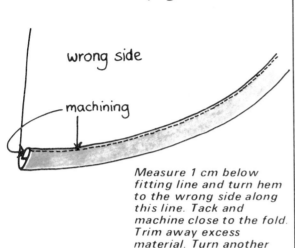

wrong side

machining

Measure 1 cm below fitting line and turn hem to the wrong side along this line. Tack and machine close to the fold. Trim away excess material. Turn another hem on the fitting line. Tack and machine, or tack and slip-hem into position. Press.

AN EDGE STITCHED PLAIN HEM ⑦

tacking

machining

slip hemming

wrong side

Turn the raw edge under. Tack and machine close to the fold. Trim turning. Tack the machined edge to the garment and slip-hem into position. Remove tacking thread and press well on the wrong side.

⑧ A FALSE HEM

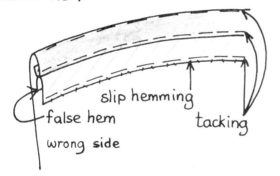

slip hemming

false hem

tacking

wrong side

Let down hem. Press the hem out flat. Mark position of new fitting line with tacking stitches. Use crossway strips of matching material for false hem [up to 8 cm in width]. Tack and machine strip to hem, right sides together. Press seam open. Turn up to the new fitting line and tack hem into position. Press lightly. Turn under raw edge. Tack and then slip-hem. Press well on the wrong side.

A BONDED HEM (using a fusible tape) ⑨

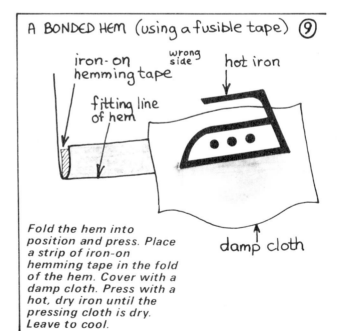

iron-on hemming tape

wrong side

hot iron

fitting line of hem

damp cloth

Fold the hem into position and press. Place a strip of iron-on hemming tape in the fold of the hem. Cover with a damp cloth. Press with a hot, dry iron until the pressing cloth is dry. Leave to cool.

allowance, or where a garment needs lengthening. Very bulky fabrics can be finished with this method, using a lightweight fabric for the false hem.

7 A non-sew iron-on hemming strip can be used for fabrics which are not affected by a hot iron. Always test a fusible hemming strip on a small piece of your fabric before starting to hem.

Crossway facings and bindings

It is not always possible to turn a flat hem on a shaped edge and usually an extra piece of material has to be used. Strips of material which are used for edging should be cut on the cross or true bias. Crossway strips will lie flat when stretched to follow a curve.

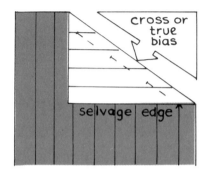

How to cut crossway strips

1 Fold the material so that one of the selvage edges lies parallel to the weft threads.
2 The diagonal fold formed will be on the cross or true bias of the material.
3 Pin the fold in position and cut through the fold.
4 Cut 3 cm-wide strips parallel to this edge.

How to join crossway strips

1 Cut the ends so that they all face the same way.
2 Crossway strips should be joined on the straight thread of the material.
3 Lay two strips at right angles to each other, with right sides inside. A sharp point should project at each end of the seam. Pin in position.
4 Stitch parallel to the straight thread of the material.
5 Press the seam open and trim the edges of the strips.

Crossway strips can be used for facing and binding shaped edges, such as collarless neck edges, sleeveless armholes, seams, or hem edges. They can also be used for attaching collars and cuffs, and for giving a decorative finish to a garment. A facing covers one side of an edge only but a binding covers both sides equally.

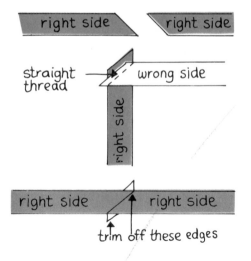

How to apply a crossway facing

1 When cutting a crossway facing strip, measure the width of facing required plus 2 cm for turnings. Join strips until you get the length required.

2 Press the outer edge of the crossway strip with a warm iron. This will help the strip to lie flat when following the curve of the shaped edge.

3 Pin and tack the facing to the garment, right sides touching. Check that the stretched edge of the crossway strip is placed over the wider part of the curved edge, for example, the outer edge of a convex curve or the inner edge of a concave curve.

4 Join the strips on the straight thread.

5 Machine the strips on the fitting line.

6 Remove tacking stitches and trim the turnings. Press open.

7 Turn the facing to the wrong side along the fitting line.

8 Fold under 1 cm turning. Pin and tack in position.

9 Sew the facing with a slip-hemming stitch.

This will make an inconspicuous facing on the wrong side of the garment. To make a conspicuous facing on the right side of the garment, work with the right side of the facing on the wrong side of the garment. The facing can be machined in place or embroidered with a decorative stitch.

How to apply a crossway binding

1 Use 3 cm wide crossway strips. Join strips until you get the length required.

2 Press the outer edge of the crossway strip with a warm iron. This will help the strip to lie flat when following the curve of the shaped edge.

3 Pin and tack the binding to the garment, right sides facing. Check that the stretched edge of the crossway strip is placed over the wider part of the curved edge, for example, the outer edge of a convex curve or the inner edge of a concave curve.

4 Machine the crossway strip on the fitting line.

5 Remove tacking stitches and trim the turnings. Press flat with the thumb.

6 Turn the binding to the wrong side.

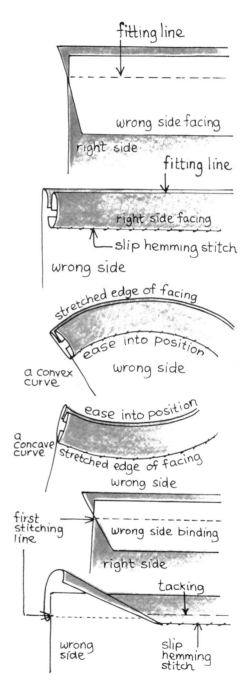

7 Fold under 1 cm turning. Pin and tack in position.
8 Slip-hem the binding to the back of the machine stitching.

Crossway binding can also be applied double thickness. The crossway strip should be folded in half lengthways, wrong sides inside, and the double strip of binding tacked and sewn to the right side of the garment. The folded edge of the binding is then taken up and over the raw edge, and slip-hemmed on the wrong side of the garment.

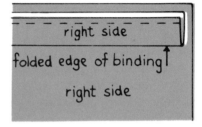
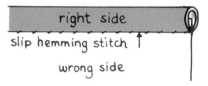

How to make shaped facings

A shaped facing can be used to finish necklines, armholes, and openings. A shaped facing is cut the same shape as the edge it is to fit. It can be finished on the wrong side of the garment to make an inconspicuous facing, or it can be made from contrasting material and turned on to the right side of the garment to make a decorative, conspicuous facing.

To face an armhole:

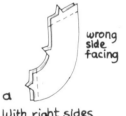
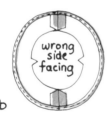
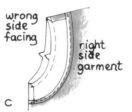
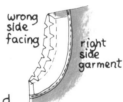

a With right sides together join facing pieces at shoulder and underarm.

b Fold and machine a 6mm turning to the wrong side around outer edge of facing.

c Matching balance marks, pin, tack and machine facing to the right side of the garment.

d Cut V-shaped notches around armhole.

e Turn facing to the wrong side of the garment. Anchor facing with hemming stitches at shoulder and underarm seams.

To face a round neckline:

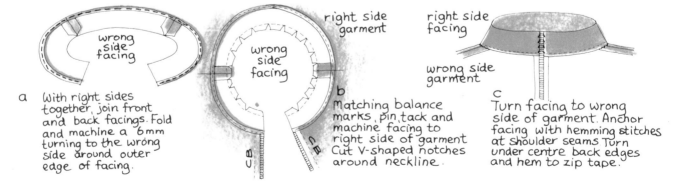

a With right sides together, join front and back facings. Fold and machine a 6mm turning to the wrong side around outer edge of facing.

b Matching balance marks, pin, tack and machine facing to right side of garment. Cut V-shaped notches around neckline.

c Turn facing to wrong side of garment. Anchor facing with hemming stitches at shoulder seams Turn under centre back edges and hem to zip tape.

To face a square neckline:

a
Prepare facings.
Matching balance
marks, pin, tack, and
machine facings to
right side of garment.
Snip into corners of
neckline and around
curved edge.

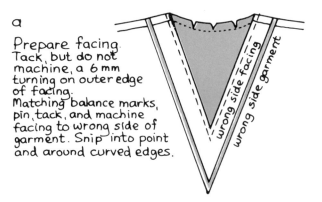

b
Turn facing to
wrong side of
garment. On the
right side edge
stitch around
neckline.

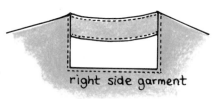

To make a decorative, conspicuous facing:

a

Prepare facing.
Tack, but do not
machine, a 6 mm
turning on outer edge
of facing.
Matching balance marks,
pin, tack, and machine
facing to wrong side of
garment. Snip into point
and around curved edges.

b
Turn facing to
right side of
garment. Tack
folded edge in
place. Pin and tack
edge of facing to
garment. Stitch
along both edges
of facing strip.

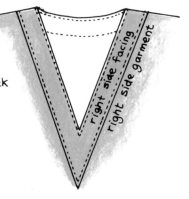

A word about waist edges

A gathered skirt can be attached to a waistband by the method described on page 122 of this chapter. To give a firm waistband that will not stretch during wear it is necessary to stiffen the band with a strong interfacing, or to insert a length of petersham inside the waist edge of the skirt. A waistband is attached after the side seams and opening have been finished, but before the hem is completed.

1 Cut the waistband, using the correct pattern piece.

2 Cut the interfacing, the length of the waistband plus $\frac{1}{2}$ cm, by the width of the waistband.

3 Iron on or tack the interfacing to the wrong side of the waistband.

4 With right sides together, fold lengthways. Pin and tack

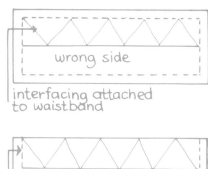

interfacing attached
to waistband

machine down ends
of waistband

along the ends of the waistband. Machine on the fitting line.

5 Trim the ends and cut across the corners. Press. Turn the waistband to the right side, carefully easing out the corners.

6 Tack around the outer edges to hold the waistband in shape.

7 With right sides together, pin and tack the front interfaced piece of the waistband to the waist edge of the skirt. Remember to match all balance marks. The waistband should be level with the opening on the front of the skirt. The extension of the waistband will project on the back side of the opening.

8 Machine on the fitting line. Trim the turnings to 1 cm.

9 Press the waistband upwards and over to the wrong side of the garment.

10 Fold under the raw edges of the waistband and tack in position.

11 Hem the folded edge to the machine stitching.

12 The completed waistband can be trimmed with machine stitching all round the edges, if required.

13 Attach hooks and bars, a special skirt hook with bar, a small piece of Velcro, or a button with worked button-hole.

Petersham can be inserted to the inside of a waist edge to form a hidden waistband. This method is particularly suitable for thick tweed fabrics because it gives a smooth waistline that is not bulky.

1 Cut a length of petersham to the waist measurement plus 5 cm.

2 Press the petersham with a hot iron and damp cloth. While still damp, stretch the lower edge into a curve. Dry with the iron. To prevent the petersham stretching, machine along the top edge. Turn under $2\frac{1}{2}$ cm at each end. Hem stitch turnings in position.

3 Attach two hooks and eyes to the ends of the band.

4 With right side of petersham against wrong side of skirt, tack the shorter curve of the petersham to the skirt waist edge. Machine along the edge of the petersham.

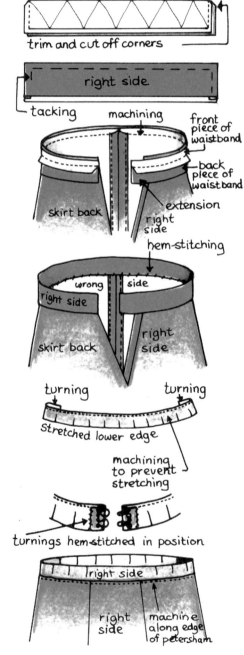

5 Trim the raw edges to $\frac{1}{2}$ cm. Using straight seam binding, cover the raw waist edge on the right side of the skirt. Tack, and machine or hem stitch along both edges of the binding.

6 Turn the waistband down on to the wrong side of the skirt. Tack along the waist edge.

7 Neaten the edges of the binding and petersham with two strips of seam binding hemmed into position.

8 Either machine round the folded edge at the top of the skirt, or catch-stitch the lower edge of the petersham to the skirt at seams and darts.

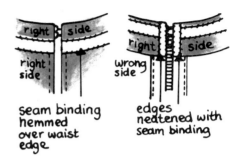

seam binding hemmed over waist edge

edges neatened with seam binding

Think and Do

1. Explain how you would cut, join, and use crossway strips to form a binding on a convex curve.

2. Draw diagrams to show how you would work bar and arrowhead tacks. For what purposes are they used in dressmaking?

3. Name three ways of dealing with fullness in a garment.

4. What is the difference between:
a. pleats and tucks;
b. binding and facing;
c. obvious and hidden waistbands?

5. Say how you would:
a. finish off a dart that is tapered at both ends;
b. level a hem;
c. gather, using a sewing machine.

6. Say what is meant by each of the following terms:
a. true bias;
b. selvage;
c. conspicuous facing;
d. gathers;
e. Paris binding.

7. How would you finish the hem of:
a. a flared cotton skirt;
b. a nylon blouse;

c. a thick tweed skirt;

d. a child's terylene dress?

8. Copy the following sentences into your notebook. Say whether each one is *true* or *false*.

a. Strips of material that are used for edging curves should be cut on the cross or true bias.

b. When machining a gathered piece of material on to a band, the gathered piece should be uppermost.

c. A small stitch and a tight top tension should be used when gathering with a sewing machine.

d. The ends of darts should be tapered gently.

e. Pin tucks are tucks which have been pinned on the wrong side of a garment.

f. A knife pleat is formed by two inverted pleats.

9. How can material which is "cut on the cross" be used in dressmaking? Illustrate your answer where possible.

10. Copy out this crossword and complete it.

Clues across

1. A band of material which fits tightly across the shoulders of a bodice.

2. An edging which covers both sides equally.

3. A decorative way of removing fullness at the top of a skirt.

Clues down

4. A type of pleat.

5. A way of enclosing fullness in a wedge shape.

6. A tiny tuck.

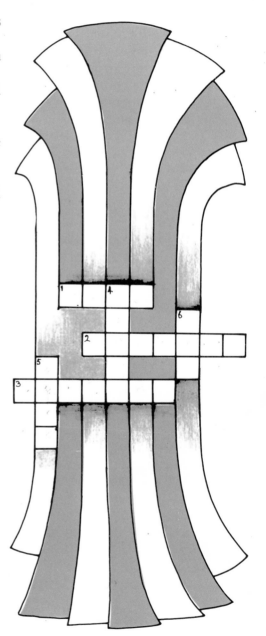

Openings

Openings are necessary so that tightly fitting garments can be put on and taken off easily. Openings are usually required at the neck, above and below the waist on side seams, and at the wrist. All openings should be:

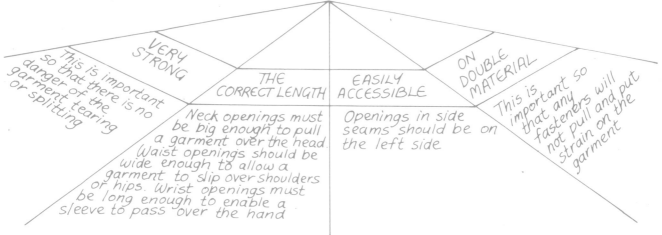

VERY STRONG
This is important so that there is no danger of the garment tearing or splitting

THE CORRECT LENGTH
Neck openings must be big enough to pull a garment over the head. Waist openings should be wide enough to allow a garment to slip over shoulders or hips. Wrist openings must be long enough to enable a sleeve to pass over the hand

EASILY ACCESSIBLE
Openings in side seams should be on the left side

ON DOUBLE MATERIAL
This is important so that any fasteners will not pull and put strain on the garment

The main types of opening are:
   a the faced slit opening;
   b the bound opening;
   c the continuous strip opening.

Faced slit opening

This opening is suitable for wrists and for neck openings.
How to make a faced slit opening on a sleeve
1 Mark the position and length of the slit with a line of tacking stitches. Do *not* cut the opening.
2 Cut a facing strip 6 to 8 cm wide, and 4 to 6 cm longer than the slit.
3 Neaten the raw edges on three sides of the facing with a machined edge stitch.
4 With right sides together, place the centre of the facing on the tacked position of the slit. Tack together.

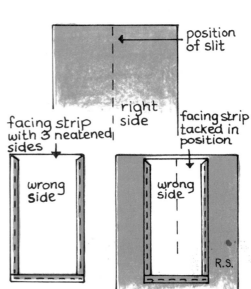

position of slit

right side

facing strip with 3 neatened sides

facing strip tacked in position

wrong side

wrong side

R.S.

5 Machine 1 cm away on either side of the tacked slit, forming a point at the bottom.

6 Remove tacking stitches and press flat.

7 Cut down the centre of the two rows of machining, as far into the point as possible.

8 Turn facing to the wrong side of the garment.

9 Tack the folded edge flat. Press well.

10 This type of opening can be reinforced with machine stitching on the right side of the garment, or the top of the loose facing can be caught down on the wrong side.

How to make a faced slit opening at the neck

A slit opening at the neck is usually faced with a shaped piece of material. The method is the same as for the sleeve opening. The bottom of the opening can be reinforced with a bar tack worked on the right side of the garment.

Bound opening

This opening is suitable for front and back neck openings. It can be made with a crossway strip of contrasting material if a decorative opening is required.

1 Mark the position and length of the opening with a line of tacking stitches. Do **not** cut the opening.

2 Cut a facing strip 6 to 8 cm wide, and 2 cm longer than the opening.

3 With right sides together, place the centre of the facing on the tacked position of the opening. Tack together.

4 Machine down either side and across the bottom of the tacked opening.

5 Remove the tacking stitches and press flat.

6 Cut down the centre of the two rows of machining and snip into each corner.

7 Wrap the facing strip round the edges of the opening to the wrong side. Tack, so that the two edges of the bound opening meet edge to edge.

8 Trim the turnings on the wrong side of the garment and fold under a narrow hem.

9 Sew the folded edge of the facing to the line of machine stitching. Overcast the ends of the facing strip.

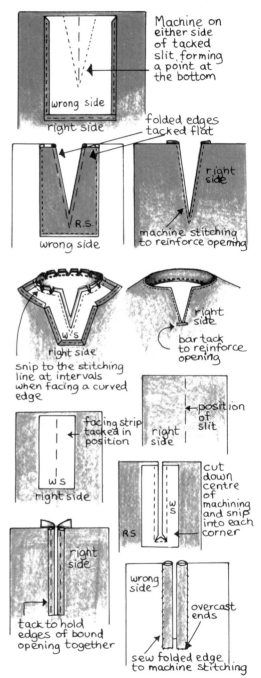

Continuous strip opening

This is a strong opening that can be used on most materials. It is formed with an underwrap and an overwrap of material, to which fasteners can be attached. A continuous strip opening can be made in a slit opening or in a seam.

1 Either cut a straight slit the length of the opening required, or cut across the seam allowance to the stitching line if the opening is to be in line with a seam.

2 Cut a strip of material on the straight thread, which is twice the length of the opening and 6 cm wide.

3 Working with the wrong side of the garment towards you, pin and tack the strip to the edge of the opening, right sides together. The garment turning will taper at the base of the opening.

4 Machine just above the tacking line, keeping the machine stitching parallel with the edge of the strip. Care must be taken at the base of the opening, where only a couple of threads on the garment will be caught in the stitching.

5 Remove the tacking stitches and press the strip away from the garment.

6 Fold the raw edge under 1 cm. Pin and tack the folded edge of the strip to meet the machine stitching on the wrong side of the garment.

7 Hem the folded edge to the machine stitching. Remove tacking.

8 Fold the opening to form an underwrap and overwrap. Press well.

9 This type of opening can be strengthened with a row of back stitch across the bottom of the opening.

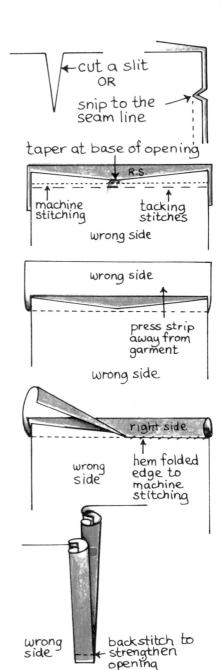

A word about dress and skirt plackets

A dress placket must open far enough to allow a tightly fitting garment to be pulled on and off the wearer easily. The closer a garment fits, the longer must be the placket. A dress placket should not be shorter than 20 cm, 10 cm above the waistline and 10 cm below. A dress placket is inserted in the left underarm seam and is not made until the bodice and skirt pieces have been joined. The usual type of fastening for a dress placket is the zip fastener (see

Chapter 15). This can be inserted by the semi-concealed or concealed methods. Both ends of the fastener should be stitched with horizontal or diagonal ends, and the tape secured to the seam allowance with slip-hemming stitches.

A skirt placket must open far enough to allow a fitted skirt to be pulled over the shoulders and hips. The length of a skirt placket is around 20 cm and the usual type of fastening is the zip fastener (see Chapter 15). A zip fastener can be inserted at the left side of a skirt using the concealed method, or into a centre front or centre back seam, using the semi-concealed method.

a dress placket showing a zip fastener sewn with horizontal ends

a dress placket showing a zip fastener sewn with diagonal ends

Think and Do

1. Name three types of opening used in dressmaking. Say where each would be used. Give instructions for working one of the methods listed.

2. Copy the following diagram into your notebook and write a suitable sentence in each of the boxes.

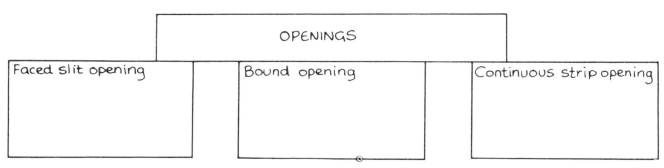

OPENINGS

| Faced slit opening | Bound opening | Continuous strip opening |

3. Which type of opening would you use for the:
a. side opening of a tweed skirt;
b. wrist opening of a long-sleeved blouse;
c. side opening of a cotton dress?

4. Prepare a classroom display of decorative openings. See how many different kinds you can collect.

5. The diagram shows the sleeve of a fitted shirt blouse. How would you face opening A?

6. Copy the following sentences into your notebook. Say whether each one is *true* or *false*.

a. Openings in a side seam should be at the right side of the wearer.

b. A slit opening at the neck is usually faced with a shaped piece of material.

c. A crossway strip is used to face a bound opening.

d. A continuous strip opening can only be made in a seam.

e. A dress placket should be made before the bodice and skirt pieces are joined.

f. The length of a skirt placket is usually 20 cm.

7. Why are openings used in dressmaking? List three important points to remember when making an opening.

8. Give instructions for making a bound opening or a continuous strip opening.

9. Say how you would:

a. make a faced slit opening on a sleeve;

b. apply a shaped facing to neaten the round neck of a dress;

c. insert a fastening in a dress placket.

10. Give instructions for:

a. strengthening the bottom of a continuous strip opening;

b. reinforcing a faced slit opening;

c. neatening the facing strip on the wrong side of a garment, when making a bound opening.

Fastenings

Fastenings can be functional, decorative or a combination of both. There are many different ways of fastening an opening.

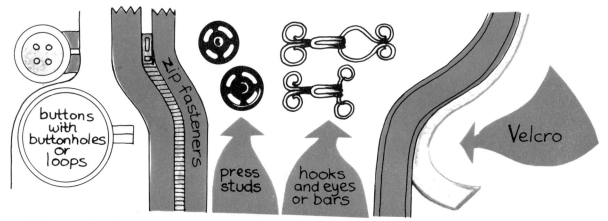

buttons with buttonholes or loops · zip fasteners · press studs · hooks and eyes or bars · Velcro

    The type of fastener chosen can make or mar a garment. Here are some general rules to help you when choosing and using fasteners.

1 Fasteners should be suitable in size and weight for the type of material being used. Fine materials need small, delicate fasteners and heavy, thick materials require larger, sturdier types.

2 Fasteners should always be sewn on double material. This ensures that the fasteners are firmly attached and that the material is not pulled or strained.

3 Unless a fastening is to be decorative, it should be as neat and inconspicuous as possible.

4 Fasteners should be evenly spaced down the length of the opening.

5 Fastenings should lie flat. There should not be any puckers or unsightly ridges when the garment is being worn.

6 All functional fastenings should be carefully and securely made, so that they will last for the lifetime of the garment.

7 Girls' and women's clothes fasten with the right side over the left. Boys' and men's clothes fasten with the left side over the right. On sleeves, the front piece usually fastens over the back.

8 The colour of the fastener should match the colour of the garment. If a perfect match is not possible when using zips or buttons, it is better to use a neutral or good contrasting colour.

Buttons

Buttons can be used for decorative as well as functional fastenings. They can be:

sewn either side of a front opening

grouped in pairs

evenly spaced

arranged in groups

used purely as a decorative feature

placed to give a double breasted effect

Buttons should be securely attached to a garment, but should not cause puckering when the garment is fastened. Some buttons have a built-in shank to allow for the thickness of the overwrapping buttonhole. When a button does not have a shank, it is necessary to work one between the button and the garment.

1 Mark the position of each button with crossed pins.

2 Join the thread by working two back stitches on the right side of the garment.

3 Place the button on top of the crossed pins.

4 Sew the button to the garment by stabbing the needle up and down through the holes of the button. The crossed pins will prevent the button from being attached to the material too tightly.

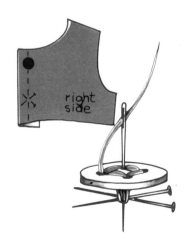

right side

5 Remove the pins and bring the thread up between the button and the garment.

6 Wind the thread firmly around the strands to form a shank.

7 Pass the thread through to the wrong side of the garment and fasten off securely with one or two back stitches.

Four-hole buttons can be sewn in the following ways:

This method forms a bulky cross and should only be used with buttons with a sunken centre

Two-hole buttons should be attached in line with the buttonhole.

a horizontal buttonhole

right side

right side

a vertical buttonhole

Fabric-covered buttons should only be used with bound buttonholes. The constant rubbing of the threads of a hand-stitched buttonhole will quickly wear away the covering.

Buttonholes

Buttonholes are slits in a garment, which have been neatened to prevent the edges from fraying. They are usually made before the buttons are sewn into position. Buttonholes are cut along a straight thread so that they will not stretch, and they are normally made on double thickness of material. Buttonholes are worked in a horizontal position, but where there is a front opening which is faced on the right side, in shirts, blouses, and dresses, they are cut and worked vertically.

a back opening with horizontal buttonholes

a front opening with vertical buttonholes

There are four kinds of buttonhole.

A worked buttonhole

This is suitable for most fabrics

A bound buttonhole

This is used on medium and heavyweight garments that are not washed frequently

A worked buttonhole loop

This is suitable for small openings that meet edge to edge without an overwrap

A rouleau or material loop

This is a strong decorative buttonhole that can be used where edges meet without an overwrap. Usually used with a small fabric-covered button

A worked horizontal buttonhole

1 Mark the length of the buttonhole with tacking stitches.
2 Using a pair of sharp scissors, cut along the length of the buttonhole.
3 Oversew the cut edges to prevent fraying.
4 Working from left to right and using a buttonhole stitch, sew along the bottom edge of the slit. (Fig. a)
5 Make a round end by fanning out the stitches. (Fig. b) On fine materials use an overcasting stitch, but thick materials can be buttonholed.
6 Work the second side of the buttonhole. (Fig. c)
7 Complete the buttonhole with a bar of stitches worked across both edges. (Fig. d)

When making a worked vertical buttonhole, both ends should match. Either work two rounded ends or finish off each end with a bar of stitches.

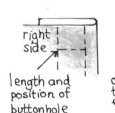

right side

length and position of buttonhole

right side

oversew the cut edges

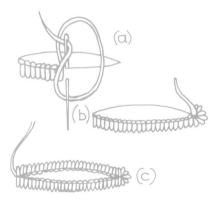

(a)

(b)

(c)

(d)

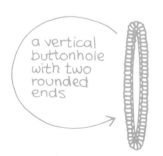

a vertical buttonhole with two rounded ends

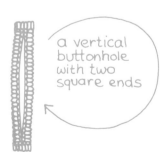

a vertical buttonhole with two square ends

Swing needle, automatic and electronic sewing machines can be used for working buttonholes. A machined buttonhole consists of a series of closed up zig-zag stitches, which are then snipped through the centre space.

a machined buttonhole

To strengthen a machined buttonhole, stitch around the buttonhole twice. A button plate can be used for machining on buttons, and instructions will be given in your sewing machine manual.

A bound buttonhole

1 Mark the length of the buttonhole with tacking stitches.
2 Cut a binding strip on the cross or true bias. It should be 5 cm wide, and 3 to 4 cm longer than the button.
3 Fold the binding strip down the centre. Lay the centre fold of the binding along the tacked position of the buttonhole, with right sides together. Tack in position.
4 On the wrong side of the binding, machine a rectangle around the buttonhole position.
5 Cut a slit down the centre of the stitching, snipping diagonally into each corner.
6 Turn the binding strip to the wrong side of garment and smooth it flat. The buttonhole should have even "lips" on the right side of the garment. Hold the edges of the opening together with tacking stitches.
7 On the wrong side, arrange the binding to form an inverted pleat at each end of the buttonhole. Hold the pleats in position with tacking stitches.
8 When the binding has been arranged correctly, tack it into position along the machine stitching. Press buttonhole flat.
9 Fold the facing to cover the back of the buttonhole. Tack in position.
10 Cut down the length of the buttonhole through the facing material.
11 Turn under the raw edges of the facing, and hem to the back of the buttonhole.

A worked buttonhole loop

1 Working on the right side of the garment, mark the position of the loop with pins. Each loop should be the width of the button.
2 Join the thread securely in the fold of the opening. Make 4 or 5 loose loops, passing backwards and forwards between the pins.

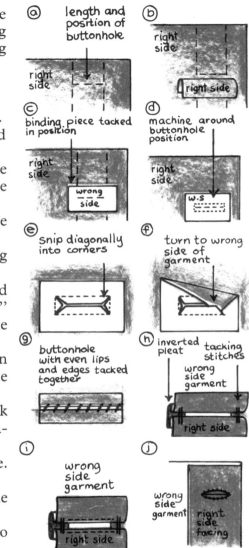

a buttonhole loop should be the width of the button

3 Work buttonhole stitch across the loop, keeping the knots facing outwards.
4 Fasten off securely on the wrong side of the garment.

A rouleau or material loop

1 Cut a crossway strip the length required and 3 cm in width.
2 Fold the strip in half, right sides facing. Tack and machine down the middle of the strip.
3 Cut one end of the rouleau to a sharp point. Thread a bodkin with a short length of strong thread, and attach firmly to the pointed end of the rouleau.
4 Push the needle inside the tube, gently turning the rouleau right side out.
5 Mark the position of the buttonhole with pins.
6 On the right side of the garment, curve the rouleau strip to form a loop between the pins, and tack into position. The loop should be the diameter of the button plus 3 cm for turnings.
7 Machine or hand sew on the fitting line.
8 With right sides together, place the facing over the loop.
9 Pin, tack and machine on the fitting line.
10 Trim the turnings and turn garment to the right side. Press well.

When making a series of loops, either cut off pieces from the rouleau the required length, or curve the rouleau to form the necessary number of loops.

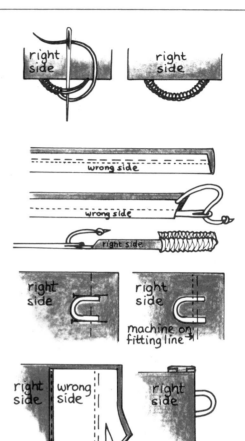

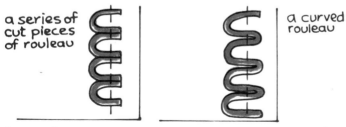

a series of cut pieces of rouleau

a curved rouleau

Hooks and eyes

Hooks and eyes are strong fasteners and can be used for openings where there is strain, for example, at waistbands and at neck edges. They are sewn on with buttonhole stitch.

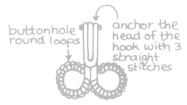

Hooks are used on the overwrap of an opening. They should be placed with the head of the hook touching the folded edge of the opening.

Eyes are used on the underwrap of an opening. Curved eyes are suitable for openings which meet edge to edge. Straight eyes are used for overlapping openings.

A worked bar tack is neat and inconspicuous, and can be used instead of a metal eye. It should be worked either on the folded edge of an opening or on the fitting line. To make a bar tack, sew 3 straight stitches and buttonhole down the length of the bar.

The top part or ball section of the press stud is sewn to the inside of the front part of the opening. Press on to the underwrap to indicate the position of the bottom part of the fastener.

The bottom part or socket section of the press stud is sewn to the back part of the opening.

Press studs

Press studs are not strong fasteners and should be used for openings where there is little strain. They can be used with hooks and eyes in dress and skirt plackets. Small press studs are oversewn into position but large press studs are firmer when worked with buttonhole stitch.

Zips

Zips vary in type and weight, and it is important to choose the correct zip for the garment you are making. Here are some points to help you when choosing and using zips.

1 Zips can have metal or nylon "teeth". Metal zips are sturdy, a feature which makes them suitable for children's clothes, but nylon zips are neat looking and less conspicuous.

2 Choose a colour of zip that will match the material you are using. If a good match cannot be found, then use a neutral colour. Sometimes a contrasting colour of zip can be a decorative feature of a garment.

3 Lightweight zips should be used for dress plackets.

4 Feather-weight zips should be used for wrist and neck openings.

5 Special skirt-weight zips should be used for skirt and trouser plackets.

6 When buying zips for cardigans, jackets, anoraks, etc. you will require the open-ended type.

7 When inserting a zip into a waist opening, the top of the zip should be level with the waist fitting line. For neck and underarm openings, the zip should be placed lower than the fitting line to leave room for a hook and eye or bar.

8 Do not stretch a seam when inserting a zip. This will give a bumpy finish.

9 When machining a zip, always use a zip presser foot attachment. This will allow you to stitch close to the seam.

10 Always press zips on the wrong side. Metal zips can be pressed well, using a damp pressing cloth, but nylon zips must only be lightly pressed.

There are two methods for inserting zips which you will use frequently in dressmaking. They are:

    a the semi-concealed;
    b the concealed methods.

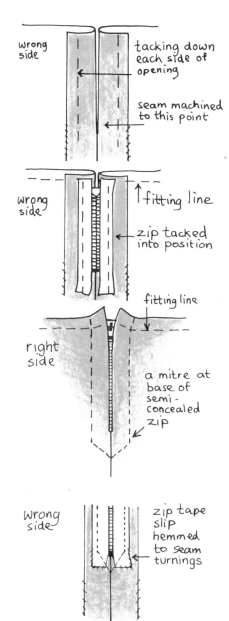

How to insert a zip into a plain seam using the semi-concealed method

This method is used when a zip is being inserted into a centre front or centre back seam. The edges of the opening meet down the centre of the zip and the stitching lines are equally spaced on either side of the seam. The plain seam must be stitched and neatened before inserting the zip.

1 Press the seam allowance flat. Tack down each side of the opening.

2 Lay the closed zip on the wrong side of the material, and pin it so that the edges of the opening meet down the centre of the zip.

3 Tack the zip into position.

4 Working on the right side of the garment, machine down one side of the opening, about $\frac{1}{2}$ cm from the seam edge. Stitch until level with the bottom of the zip.

5 Insert the machine needle into the garment, lift the presser foot, and pivot the garment so that you can machine diagonally to the seam.

6 With needle in the garment, lift the presser foot, pivot the garment, and machine a matching diagonal line on the other side of the seam. This will form a mitre.

7 Stitch up the second side of the zip, about $\frac{1}{2}$ cm from the seam edge.

8 On the wrong side of the garment, neaten across the top

and bottom of the zip, by slip-hemming the tape to the seam turnings.

How to insert a zip into a plain seam using the concealed method

This method is suitable for side plackets on skirts and for inserting open-ended zips.

1 Press the seam allowance flat.

2 Open the zip and, working on the right side of the garment, pin the outer edge of the zip teeth to the back seam edge. Pin the seam turnings and zip tape together.

3 Tack the zip firmly in position down the back seam edge.

4 Machine down the back side of the opening, about $\frac{1}{4}$ cm from the edge.

5 Close the zip. Fold the front seam edge over to meet the stitching line on the back. The front seam should then completely cover the zip teeth.

6 Pin the bottom and top of the front seam to the left half of the zip. Pin down the length of the zip, easing out any fullness in the seam.

7 Tack the zip firmly in position down the front seam edge.

8 Machine down the front side of the opening, about 1 cm from the edge.

9 When level with the bottom of the zip, insert the machine needle into the garment, lift the presser foot and pivot the garment so that you can machine diagonally to the seam.

Velcro

Velcro fastening consists of two strips of nylon material. One strip is covered with tiny hooks, while the other strip contains a series of small loops. When the two strips of material touch, the hooks intertwine with the loops and a firm fastener is formed. Velcro is useful for fastening soft furnishings, such as cushion covers and loose chair covers. Short pieces of Velcro can be used for fastening openings in clothes, for example, plackets in skirts and dresses; neck openings in dresses, blouses and tunics; front openings on anoraks, cardigans, and jackets. Velcro

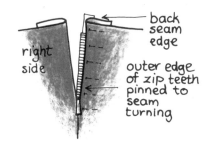

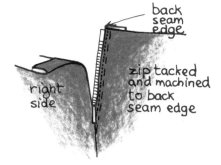

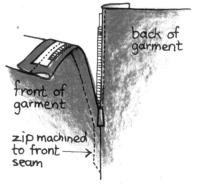

right side

is suitable for children's clothes, the simple "touch-and-close" procedure making it an easy fastening for young children to master.

Velcro can be machined or hemmed firmly in position along the edge of an opening. The soft side should be attached to the underneath of the overwrap, and the rough strip to the top of the underwrap. Always keep Velcro fastenings closed, especially during laundering. This will prevent the strip from "snagging" other clothes, and from collecting fluff and loose threads.

Think and Do

1. Name four methods of fastening a garment and say where each could be used.
2. Visit your school and local libraries and find out all you can on:
a. early types of buttons;
b. the origins of the zip fastener;
c. how "Velcro" works.
3. Prepare a collage using old, surplus fasteners.
4. How would you insert a concealed zip fastener in the side opening of a skirt?
5. What type of buttonhole would you use with fabric-covered buttons for the front opening of a tweed dress? Say how you would make the buttonholes.
6. Which means of fastening would you choose for:
a. the side opening of a pair of jeans;
b. the cuff of a long-sleeved blouse;
c. the front opening of a tunic top;
d. the side opening of a crimplene dress;
e. the back opening of a denim skirt?
7. Say how you would:
a. mitre the base of a semi-concealed zip fastening;
b. work a vertical buttonhole;
c. sew on a button that has not got a shank;
d. make a rouleau.

8. Copy the following diagram into your notebook and write a suitable sentence in each of the boxes.

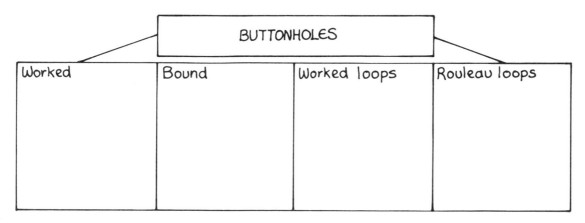

BUTTONHOLES			
Worked	Bound	Worked loops	Rouleau loops

9. Find out the current price of:
a. a 25 cm open-ended metal zip;
b. a 15 cm strip of Velcro;
c. half a dozen shirt buttons;
d. a 12 cm lightweight nylon zip.

10. Copy the following diagrams into your notebook and draw in worked buttonholes in the correct positions.

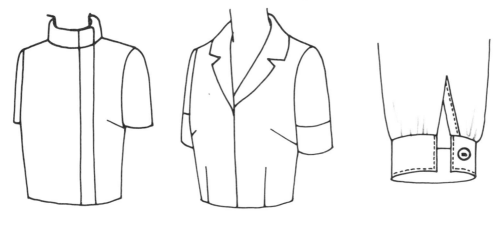

Neck finishes

A neck edge can be finished with a shaped facing or collar.

A shaped facing can be conspicuous or inconspicuous, is made after the seams have been neatened and the front or back opening completed. (See Chapter 13, page 130 for shaped facings.)

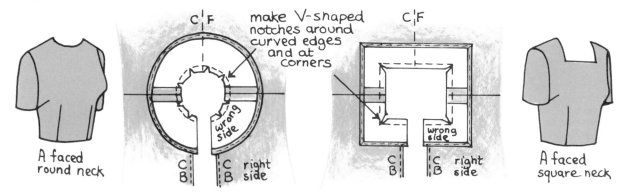

A collar can be straight or curved. It can lie flat on the shoulders, stand up around the neck or roll over.

How to make a collar

1 Tack or iron-on interfacing to the wrong side of the under collar. With right sides facing and matching fitting lines, pin and tack collar pieces together.

2 Machine round the outer edge of the collar, starting and finishing at the neck fitting line.

3 Trim the turnings to ½ cm. On heavy fabrics trim surplus material close to the stitching line. Cut across the corners

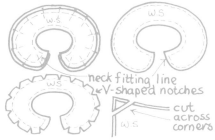

(on a straight collar) and snip V-shaped notches round the curved edge (on a Peter Pan collar).

4 Turn the collar to the right side. Pin and tack around the edge, easing the seam slightly to the underside of the collar. This will prevent the under collar from showing when the garment is being worn. Press well.

5 If a slippery fabric is being used, tack diagonally through both layers to keep the collar flat.

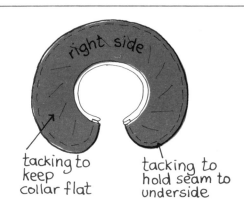

tacking to keep collar flat

tacking to hold seam to underside

How to attach a collar

A collar should be attached to a bodice before the under-arm seams are sewn and the sleeves are inserted.

There are three ways of attaching a collar.

1. A collar can be self-neatening. In this method the neck edge of the garment is inserted between an over-collar and an under-collar. The under-collar is hemmed to the machine stitching around the neck edge, on the right side of the garment. A facing is not required.	*2. A collar can be attached using a shaped facing, which usually extends to neaten the front opening of the bodice. This method is suitable for straight or curved collars.*	*3. A collar can be attached using a crossway strip as a facing. This method is not suitable for collars which are worn open, because the facing strip would be obvious.*

A straight self-neatening collar

1 Neaten the raw edge on the front facing.

2 With the right side of the garment towards you, fold the facing back. Pin and tack in position.

3 Machine along the fitting line of the neck edge to the centre front positions. (These will be indicated on the paper pattern by a notch or perforation.)

4 Snip down to the stitching line at the centre front positions, and trim the turnings and corners to $\frac{1}{4}$ cm.

5 Turn facings to the wrong side. Press. Pin and tack down the centre front lines.

6 With the wrong side of the garment facing you, pin the top of the collar in position around the neck edge. The edges of the collar should start and finish on the centre front lines.

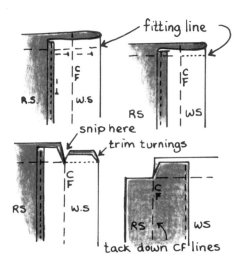

fitting line

snip here

trim turnings

tack down CF lines

7 Tack the top of the collar to the neck fitting line. The collar may need to be eased into position, but do check that the ends of the collar are on the centre front lines, and that the centre back of the collar matches the centre back of the bodice.

8 Machine on the fitting line. Trim the turnings to $\frac{1}{2}$ cm, and snip around the curved edge. Turn the collar up and press well.

9 On the right side of the garment, fold under the turnings on the under collar. Pin and tack the folded edge to the machined fitting line.

10 Hem the under collar to the machine stitching. Press.

A collar with a shaped facing

1 With the right side of the garment facing you, pin the collar in position, top side uppermost. Match balance marks and fitting lines, and check that the ends of the collar are on the centre front lines.

2 Tack along the neck fitting line.

3 Prepare the shaped facing by joining the back and front neck pieces at the shoulders. Trim the turnings and press the seam open. Neaten the outer edge of the facing.

4 With right sides together, put the shaped facing over the collar and bodice sections. Match balance marks and fitting lines. Pin, tack, and machine up the front of the opening, along the neck edge and down the other side of the opening.

5 Trim the turnings to $\frac{1}{2}$ cm. Make V-shaped notches along the curved neck edge and trim off the corners.

6 Fold the facing to the wrong side of the garment, carefully easing out the corners.

7 Tack up the front of the opening, along the base of the collar, and down the other side of the opening. Press well.

8 Hem the facing to the shoulder seams.

A collar with a crossway strip

1 With the right side of the garment facing you, pin the collar in position, top side uppermost. Match balance marks and fitting lines, and check that the ends of the collar are on the centre front lines.

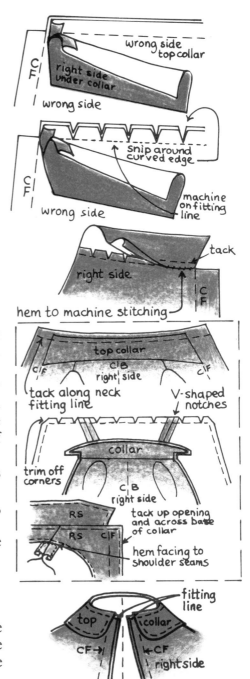

2 Tack along the neck fitting line.

3 Neaten the raw edges of the centre front facing, and fold the facing extension on to the right side of the garment to enclose the ends of the collar.

4 Cut a 3 cm wide crossway strip. With the right side of the crossway strip facing the collar and garment, pin and tack the upper raw edge of the strip about $\frac{1}{2}$ cm above the fitting line. The strip should overlap the folded facing at each side.

5 Machine on the fitting line.

6 Trim the turnings to $\frac{1}{2}$ cm. Make V-shaped notches along the curved neck edge.

7 Press the crossway strip up and over on to the wrong side of the garment. Carefully ease out the corners of the facing.

8 Tack along the base of the collar to hold the strip in position.

9 Turn under the raw edge of the crossway strip. Tack the folded edge flat on to the garment, stretching the crossway strip slightly.

10 Hem the folded edge of the strip to the garment, and the front facing to the crossway strip.

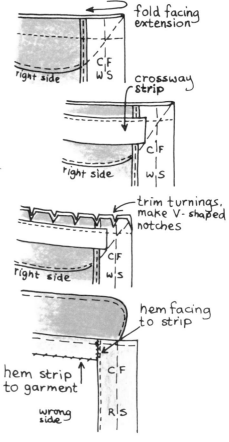

A word about interfacings

Interfacing or interlining is used to:

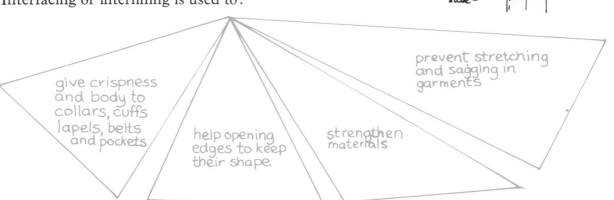

give crispness and body to collars, cuffs lapels, belts and pockets

help opening edges to keep their shape

strengthen materials

prevent stretching and sagging in garments

There are two types of interfacing:

    a woven;

    b non-woven or bonded.

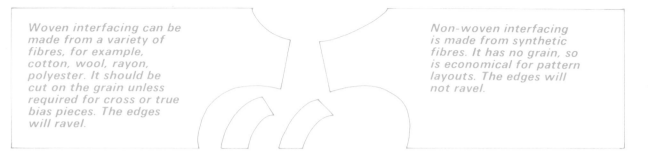

Woven interfacing can be made from a variety of fibres, for example, cotton, wool, rayon, polyester. It should be cut on the grain unless required for cross or true bias pieces. The edges will ravel.

Non-woven interfacing is made from synthetic fibres. It has no grain, so is economical for pattern layouts. The edges will not ravel.

Woven and non-woven interfacings can be attached to material by:

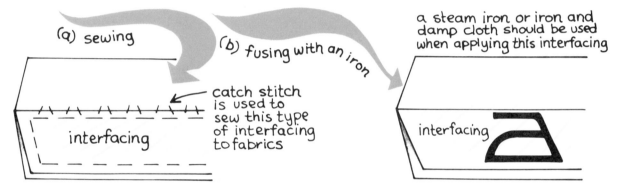

(a) sewing

(b) fusing with an iron

catch stitch is used to sew this type of interfacing to fabrics

interfacing

a steam iron or iron and damp cloth should be used when applying this interfacing

interfacing

When chosen and used with care, interfacing can improve the look and feel of a garment. If, however, you prefer a garment that has a soft, natural or draped appearance, you may choose not to use interfacing.

Here are some general points to help you if choosing and using interfacing.

1 Choose the right weight of interfacing. It should not be heavier than the material you are using.

2 An interfacing should not show through a material. For very fine fabrics, a lawn or silk organza interfacing is best.

3 Do check that you choose a washable interfacing for a washable garment.

4 If you are using an iron-on interfacing, read the manufacturer's instructions carefully. Use this type of interfacing only for small areas, such as collars and cuffs.

Large areas of iron-on interfacing can become detached from the fabric.

5 When interfacing pieces of fabric which are cut on the cross, remember to use woven interfacing. Non-woven interfacing will not stretch.

6 Do not apply iron-on interfacing over pins or tacking. You will not be able to remove them.

7 Use a stretch interfacing for knitted materials.

Think and Do

1. Copy the following diagrams into your notebook and name each type of collar.

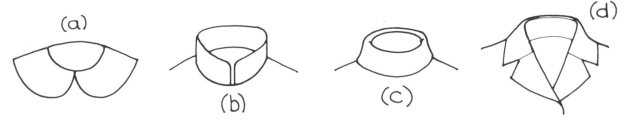

(a)   (b)   (c)   (d)

2. Say how you would apply a straight collar to a blouse with a faced front opening.

3. Copy the following diagram into your notebook and write a suitable sentence in each of the boxes.

WAYS OF ATTACHING A COLLAR		
The self neatening method	Using a shaped facing	Using a crossway strip

4. Why is interfacing used in dressmaking? What points should be considered when choosing and using interfacing?

5. In your notebook explain the difference between:

a. woven and non-woven interfacing;

b. fusible and non-fusible interfacing.

6. With the aid of diagrams, describe how you would make up this collar.

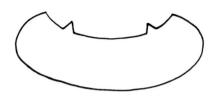

7. In your notebook, say how you would:

a. attach a collar with a crossway strip;

b. apply a fusible interfacing;

c. prepare the front opening of a blouse for a straight, self-neatening collar.

8. Copy the following sentences into your notebook. Say whether each one is *true* or *false*.

a. A woven interfacing should be cut on the grain.

b. V-shaped notches should be cut along curved edges to make them lie flat.

c. A collar should not be attached to a bodice before the sleeves have been inserted.

d. A fusible interfacing is suitable for large areas.

e. When making a conspicuous shaped neck facing, the facing should be machined to the right side of the bodice and then turned to the wrong side.

f. A sewn-in interfacing is fastened to the fabric with catch stitch.

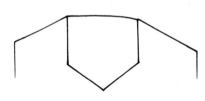

9. Collect magazine cuttings of dresses, blouses, and tunic tops. Stick them neatly into your notebook and underneath each one name the type of neck finish used.

10. Say how you would neaten this neck edge.

Sleeves

Sleeves should be made up before they are set into the bodice section. This means that:

    a openings,
    b elbow darts,
    c sleeve seams,
    d wrist or lower edges of sleeves,

must all be completed.

Openings

Full sleeves which fit into a cuff or wristband and long, close-fitting sleeves will require an opening. The position of the opening will be marked on the paper pattern.

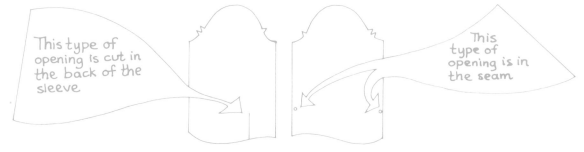

A faced or continuous strip opening can be used (see Chapter 14).

Elbow darts

Sew any elbow darts before the sleeve seams are joined. Elbow darts are pressed downwards.

Sleeve seams

Sew the sleeve seams with the same type of seam that you are using for the rest of the garment. This will usually be a plain seam, but a french or machine-felled seam may be used if more suitable. Remember to match balance marks and fitting lines before sewing seams. Plain seams should be pressed open and neatened.

Wrist or lower edge of sleeves

Full sleeves can be finished with a simple cuff, or faced with a casing which is then threaded with elastic.

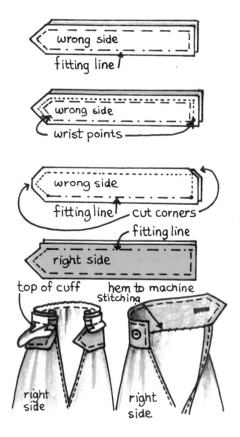

To make a simple self-neatening cuff with an opening

1 With right sides facing and matching fitting lines, pin and tack the cuff pieces together.

2 Machine round the outer edge of the cuff, starting and finishing on the wrist points.

3 Trim the turnings to $\frac{1}{2}$ cm and cut across the corners.

4 Turn cuff to the right side. Pin and tack round the edge. Press well.

5 Gather the lower edge of the sleeve. Pull up the gathering threads until the sleeve fits the cuff.

6 With the right side of the sleeve towards you, pin the top side of the cuff to the sleeve edge.

7 Tack the top of the cuff to the sleeve edge, and machine on the fitting line.

8 Trim the turnings to $\frac{1}{2}$ cm. Turn the cuff up and press well.

9 On the wrong side of the garment, turn under the raw edge of the cuff. Pin, tack, and hem the folded edge on to the machine stitching.

10 To fasten the cuff, use a button and worked buttonhole, or a small piece of Velcro.

To make a simple cuff without an opening

1 Join the ends of the cuff together with a plain seam. Press open.

2 With right sides together, pin and tack the cuff along the sleeve edge. Position the cuff so that the cuff and sleeve seams match.

3 Machine on the fitting line.

4 Trim the turnings to $\frac{1}{2}$ cm. Turn the cuff downwards and press well.

5 Working on the wrong side of the sleeve, turn under the raw edge of the cuff. Pin and tack the folded edge to the fitting line.

6 Hem the folded edge to the machine stitching.

To face a sleeve edge with a casing

1 Cut a crossway strip, the length of the sleeve edge plus 2 cm, and $1\frac{1}{2}$ cm wider than the elastic.

2 Fold under the seam allowance at each end of the crossway strip. Tack in place.

3 With right sides facing, pin and tack the crossway strip to the sleeve edge. Position the strip so that the folded ends meet at the sleeve seam.

4 Machine along the fitting line.

5 Trim the turnings to $\frac{1}{2}$ cm. Turn the casing strip down and press well.

6 On the wrong side of the sleeve, tack through the sleeve and casing to hold the seam on the edge.

7 Turn under the raw edge of the casing. Pin and tack flat to the sleeve.

8 Machine or hem along the edge of the casing.

9 Thread a piece of elastic through the casing. Stitch the ends firmly together.

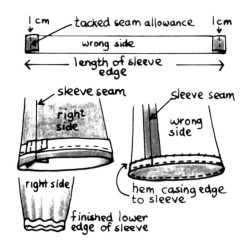

If the sleeve edge is curved or the fabric bulky, a casing must be made with a crossway strip. If the edge is straight and the fabric fine, a casing can be made with the hem allowance.

When you have completed each sleeve, then you are ready to set the sleeves into the bodice.

To insert a sleeve with a plain seam

1 Make two rows of running stitches round the head of the sleeve, one each side of the seam line. You may wish to use a machine gathering stitch for this purpose.

2 Carefully pull up the gathering threads, distributing the gathers evenly. Wrap the ends of the threads round a pin.

3 With right sides together, place the sleeve against the armhole, checking that you are using the right sleeve with the right armhole. Matching side seams and balance marks, pin the sleeve to the bodice. You may need to tighten or loosen the gathering threads to obtain a good fit, but do see that the gathers are evenly distributed.

4 Using small stitches, tack the sleeve to the bodice along the fitting line.

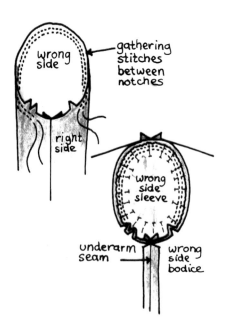

5 Before machining, try on the garment and make any necessary adjustments.

6 Working with the sleeve uppermost, machine on the fitting line. Overlap the machining for about 5 cm around the underarm seam. This will strengthen the part which takes the most strain.

7 Remove gathering and tacking thread. Trim the turnings to ½ cm and oversew or buttonhole the two edges together. On fine fabrics, make two rows of machining and trim the turnings to the first row of stitches.

8 Press the sleeve carefully using a sleeve board.

This type of sleeve can also be inserted with a french or machine-felled seam.

To insert a raglan sleeve

This type of sleeve is set into the bodice with two seams which run from the underarm to the neck. The top of the sleeve becomes the shoulder part of the bodice. For this reason, a raglan sleeve is attached to the bodice before the sleeve is made up.

1 Sew the dart at the head of the sleeve. Slit the dart open if necessary, and press flat. Oversew the dart edges.

2 With right sides facing and matching balance marks, pin and tack the front and back armhole seams to the bodice.

3 Machine along the fitting lines.

4 Trim the turnings to ½ cm. Make V-shaped notches along the curved edges, so that the seams will lie flat.

5 Press seams open and oversew or buttonhole the raw edges.

6 Matching balance marks, pin, tack and machine the underarm and side seams, along the fitting lines. (A piece of tape can be used to strengthen the curved underarm seam. If using strengthening tape, tack it in position before the seam is sewn.)

7 Snip at each side of the curved seam, so that it will lie flat. Neaten the raw edges.

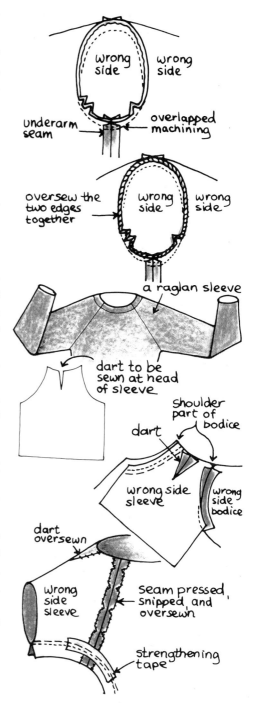

To insert a magyar sleeve without a gusset

This type of sleeve is cut in one with the bodice section. It has a curved underarm seam but no shoulder seam.

1 With right sides together and matching balance marks, pin and tack the sleeve/side seam of the garment, along the fitting line. A piece of strengthening tape can be tacked along the curved underarm seam before the seam is sewn. Machine on the fitting line.

2 Snip at each side of the curved seam, so that it will lie flat. Neaten the raw edges.

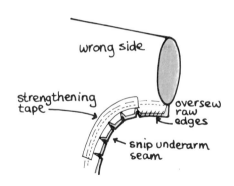

Think and Do

1. In your notebook say how you would prepare and attach an elastic casing to the lower edge of this sleeve.

2. How would you set in a sleeve with a plain seam?

3. List the various stages involved in the making of this sleeve. Place the processes in the correct order.

4. Copy the following diagram into your notebook and write a suitable sentence in each of the boxes.

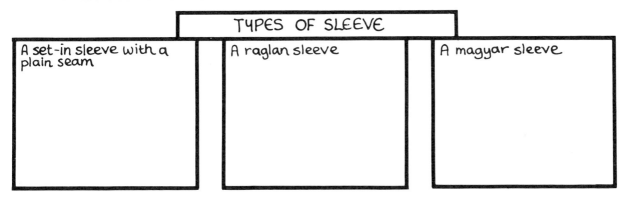

TYPES OF SLEEVE

A set-in sleeve with a plain seam

A raglan sleeve

A magyar sleeve

5. Why were the following sleeves so named? Use your school and local libraries and try to trace their origins.
a. Raglan sleeves;
b. Bishop sleeves;
c. Magyar sleeves.
6. How would you make and attach the cuff of a long-sleeved shirt blouse that has an opening?
7. Identify the sleeve below, and in your notebook say how you would attach it to a bodice.

8. In your notebook say how you would:
a. strengthen a curved underarm seam;
b. make a simple cuff without an opening;
c. gather a sleeve head.
9. Find out how sleeves have changed through the centuries. Choose one style which you like and sketch it in your notebook. Say when it would have been worn and by whom.

10. Copy out this crossword and complete it.

Clues across

1. This type of sleeve is set into the bodice with two seams.
2. A long close-fitting sleeve will require this.
3. A type of sleeve.

Clues down

4. This can be used to strengthen curved underarm seams.
5. Elastic is threaded through this.
6. Sleeves are usually inserted with this type of seam.

About trims

Care and attention must be given to the trimming and finishing touches of a garment. It is these which will help to create that professional look, for which every home dressmaker strives. Always take your time during the vital finishing stages. The temptation is to consider the garment almost finished. This can be disastrous and can lead to rushed and careless work, so **be patient**.

Belts

Belts can be stiffened or unstiffened. A stiffened belt can be made in the same way as the interfaced waistband (see page 131, Chapter 13), but with one pointed end. When the belt is turned to the right side, the raw edges should be turned under and the folds hem stitched together. A buckle should be attached to the square end of the belt and metal eyelet holes inserted at the pointed end, using a special eyelet tool.

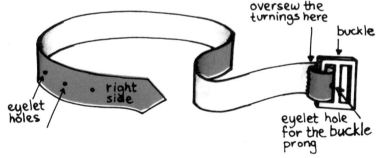

How to make an unstiffened belt

1 With right sides facing, fold the strip lengthways.
2 Pin, tack, and machine along the fitting line, leaving an 8 cm gap down the long side.
3 Trim the turnings and cut across points and corners. Using the gap, turn the belt to the right side.
4 Turning under the raw edges of the gap, hem stitch the folds together. Press.

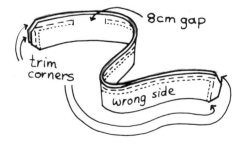

5 An unstiffened belt can be edged with machine stitching, if required.

Belt carriers

These are used to hold belts in position. They can be worked in thread or made with fabric. A thread belt carrier is worked in the same way as a buttonhole loop (see page 144, Chapter 15). It should be the width of the belt plus 1 cm, and is worked on the right side of the garment, above and below the waist seam.

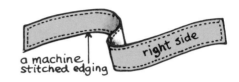

How to make a fabric belt carrier

1 Cut out a strip, 2 cm in width and 3 cm longer than the width of the belt.

2 With right sides together, fold the strip lengthways.

3 Pin, tack, and machine down the length of the strip. Trim the turnings and turn the strip to the right side (see **making a rouleau**, page 145, Chapter 15). Press.

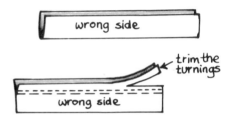

4 Edge with machine stitching, if liked.

5 Turn under 1 cm at each end of the strip. Press.

6 Pin the belt carrier over the side seam, centrally in position across the waist seam. Allow for the thickness of the belt by giving ease to the carrier.

7 Either hem securely across the folded ends of the carrier, or work a square of machining at each end.

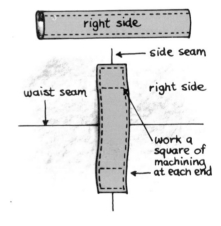

Pockets

Pockets should be large enough to be useful, unless they are being added purely as a decorative feature. They should be neatly and securely attached to a garment.

How to make a patch pocket

1 Neaten the top edge of the pocket. This can be done by hemming, facing, or binding.

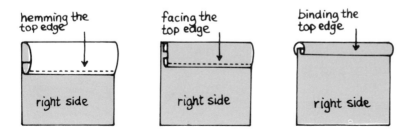

2 Turn the remaining edges of the pocket to the wrong side along the fitting line, and tack in position. Press. Trim the turnings and cut V-shaped notches around curved edges. Form pleats with the fullness at corners and points.

3 Lay the pocket on the right side of the garment, matching fitting lines. Pin and tack in position.

4 Machine the pocket to the garment. Strengthen the top corners by machining a triangle or rectangle. A double row of machining can be used to enclose the raw edges of the turnings.

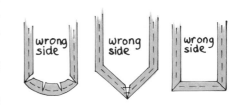

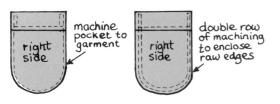

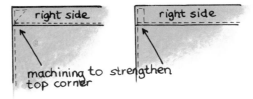

Trimming with lace

Lace can be made from cotton, nylon or a nylon/rayon mixture. It can be:

a knitted and crocheted, for example, raschel knitted lace, curtain lace;

b woven, for example, Leavers lace;

c embroidered, for example, guipure lace, broderie anglaise.

Lace can be used as *a* an edging trim; *b* an insertion; *c* an all over fabric.

How to trim with lace edging

1 Neaten the raw hem edge of the garment. This can be done using a zig-zag machine stitch, oversewing by hand, or making a narrow machined hem.

2 If the lace edging is to be gathered, draw up the strong gathering thread at the edge of the lace, to the required length.

3 Working on the right side of the garment, lay the flat or gathered lace edging over the neatened hem. Pin and tack in position.

4 Attach the lace edging to the garment with a zig-zag machine stitch, a back stitch, an embroidery stitch or with oversewing. Press.

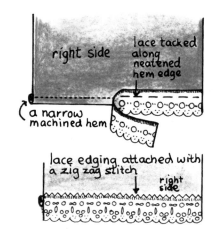

How to make a lace insertion

1 Working on the right side of the garment, lay the lace edging centrally over the seam. Pin and tack in position.

2 Using a zig-zag machine stitch, sew down each side of the insertion strip.

3 Trim away the seam and fabric on the wrong side of the garment, being careful not to cut into the lace.

4 A lace edging can also be inserted parallel with the hem. To do this, measure up from the hem edge and mark the required position of the lace with tacking stitches.

5 Lay the lace over the tacking stitches. Pin and tack.

6 Attach the lace with a machine zig-zag stitch.

7 Trim away the fabric on the wrong side of the garment.

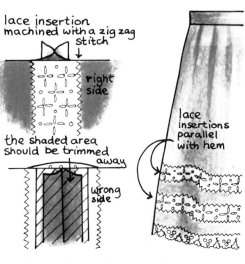

Making and attaching frills

Frills can be used to add decoration to a garment or to add length. They can be used to trim neck lines, sleeve edges, and hems. Frills can be cut in single or double width material, and can vary in fullness.

1 Cut the required lengths of fabric and join the pieces together with a plain seam.

2 Neaten the hem edge of the frill, using the hemming attachment on a machine. Fine frills can be neatened with a double row of machine zig-zag stitch.

3 Either use the frilling attachment on a machine to gather and stitch the frill in position, or :

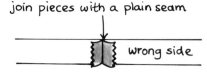
join pieces with a plain seam

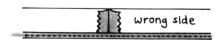
a narrow machined hem

a gather the frill with a double row of machine gathering stitches;

b with right sides together, sew the frill to the hem edge;

c neaten the hem/frill edges using a zig-zag, over-sewing, or blanket stitch.

4 If a frill will not lie flat when pressed, machine around the edge of the hem on the right side of the garment.

5 A frill can be attached using an overlaid seam.

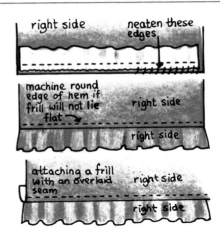

Trimming with braid

Braid can be used to add decoration or to give a new look to an old garment. It can be bound on to edges or applied flat to a garment as a surface decoration.

How to bind with braid

1 On the right side of the garment, pin and tack the braid so that half the width of the braid projects over the edge. Mitre corners (see how to apply flat braid).

2 Machine along the tacked edge of the braid.

3 Turn the unstitched edge of the braid to the wrong side of the garment. Pin and tack in position.

4 Using small, firm hemming stitches, sew the braid to the row of machining. Oversew the edges of mitred corners.

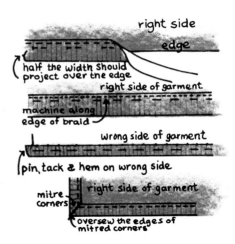

braid used to trim a neckline

How to apply flat braid

1 When flat braid is to run parallel to an edge, for example, at hem or neck lines, measure up/down from the edge and mark the required position of the braid with tacking stitches.

2 Lay the braid over the tacking stitches. Pin and tack firmly down both edges of the braid.

3 Mitre corners. Light- and medium-weight braids of a narrow width can have folded mitres. Heavy, wide braids should have stitched mitres.

4 Back stitch or machine stitch close to the edges of the braid.

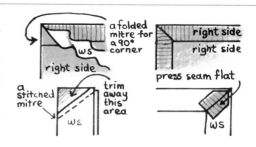

Think and Do

1. The illustration shows a six-gore nylon underslip. With the aid of diagrams, say how you would:

a. make lace insertions down the seams;

b. use lace edging to trim the hem.

2. Arrange a class display of "pockets". See how many different kinds, shapes and sizes you can collect.

3. Give instructions for making a stiffened belt. What would you use to hold the belt in position during wear?

4. Describe one method of trimming and adding interest to each of the following garments:

a. a blazer;

b. a nylon underskirt;

c. a cotton apron;

d. a long evening-skirt.

5. Visit your school and local libraries and find out all you can on:
a. Nottingham lace;
b. the braiding of men's clothes in the seventeenth and eighteenth centuries.
6. In your notebook, describe how you would:
a. prepare and attach a patch pocket;
b. use braiding to give a new lease of life to an old pinafore dress;
c. attach a frill to lengthen a cotton skirt.
7. Rearrange the following letters. They are all types of lace.
a. PEGIRUU;
b. SLAHRCE;
c. ARLESVE;
d. OIBEEDRR ILESAGAN;
e. TLCHLNAIY.
8. Say how you would make and attach a fabric belt carrier.
9. In your notebook, sketch a design for a lace wedding dress. What accessories would you plan to complete the outfit?
10. Have fun with a belt. Using a remnant of material, cut out and sew a soft belt. Decorate it in any way you like. Try to find an unusual fastening for your creation. Why not ask your teacher to arrange a "make a belt competition"?